HOB MOOR

Historic Stray
and
Local Nature Reserve

Elizabeth A Smith

William Sessions Limited
York, England

ISBN 1 85072 319 2

Printed in 11½ point Times Typeface
by Sessions of York
The Ebor Press
York, England

Contents

Acknowledgements

THE FRIENDS OF HOB MOOR COMMITTEE gratefully acknowledge all the help and encouragement received in the production of this book; support, commitment and goodwill have been shown by very many people, both amateur and professional, over at least four years. A list appears on page 98 but we would especially like to acknowledge the contribution of the following to the genesis, research and publication of this book: Martin Hammond, the late Geoffrey Hodgson, John Oxley, Rex Russell, Dinah Tyszka, Mark Tyszka, and the staff of York City Archives and the City of York Reference Library.

We thank also all those members of Friends of Hob Moor and others who have supported the group's activities; they too have contributed indirectly to the publication of this book. Without them, we would not have had the necessary broad base of support.

The text is by Elizabeth Smith, with contributions by Michael Allen in sections 3, 8 and 11, Margaret Weeden in section 19, and Ron Stirk in section 22. "Hob Moor: A Mysteriography" in section 25 is by Stephen Sayers.

Photographs (mostly taken on Hob Moor or Little Hob Moor) and sketch-maps are by Elizabeth Smith except where indicated otherwise.

Drawings are by Patricia Palaeologina, Swea Sayers and Mark Tyszka.

Cover photographs are by Pauline Walker.

We gratefully acknowledge a grant from Awards for All without whose help the production of this book would not have been possible. We should also like to thank the Yorkshire Philosophical Society and the Sheldon Memorial Trust for grants which they made towards the production costs of the book.

The material presented in these pages has been thoroughly researched but we would welcome any comments that would shed more light on the ecology and history of Hob Moor, and corrections for any mistakes we may have inadvertently made.

We have made strenuous efforts to trace all holders of copyright for material reproduced. We apologise to any whom we have not been able to contact.

Introduction

IT IS OUR INTENTION in publishing this book to share our enthusiasm and knowledge about the history and ecology of Hob Moor, as so far established. Doubtless, more work will be done. The sections are of varying length and each one deals with a separate topic; thus, the reader can dip in to those that appeal. There are some surprises! For example, you may not know that:

> an army was encamped on Hob Moor;
>
> there is a link between Hob Moor and the magnificent St William Window in York Minster;
>
> there was a water-mill in the north-east corner in medieval times;
>
> an aerodrome was proposed for Hob Moor;
>
> skylarks breed on Hob Moor and it is the only significant such area inside the York ringroad;
>
> Hob Moor still has the wild flowers of old pastureland.

Or you may have wondered about all those low ridges; or how long the Moor has been grazed by cattle; or even why the area is called "Hob" Moor ...

We hope you will find that this book is an informative and interesting read. There is something for everyone!

How to get to Hob Moor

THE TWO EASIEST ACCESS POINTS to Hob Moor are at the Edmund Wilson Swimming Baths, Thanet Road, where car parking is available, and opposite the Tyburn on Tadcaster Road, where there is a Toucan crossing adjacent to Pulleyn Drive.

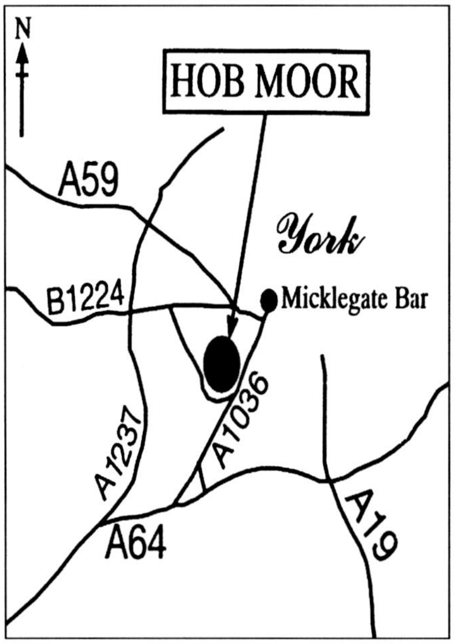

Location of Hob Moor

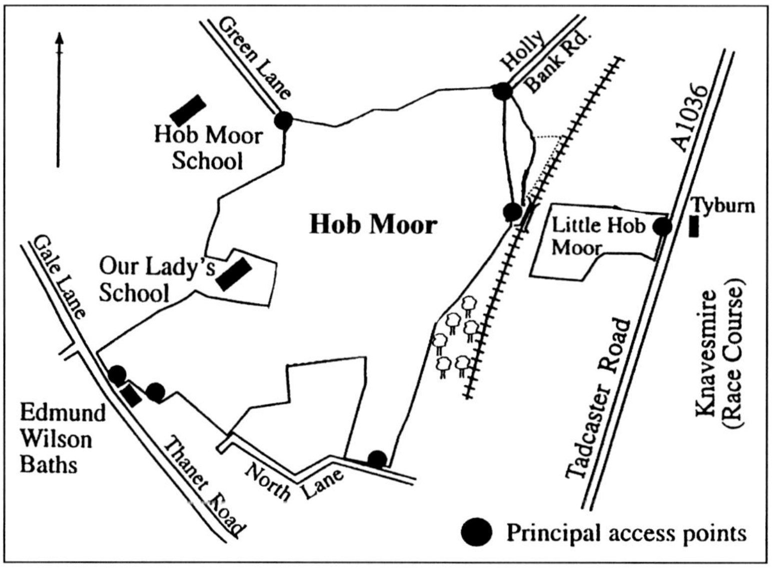

Hob Moor is about 1.5 miles (2.3km) south-west of York Minster. Its area is approximately 90 acres (36 hectares).

1. In the Beginning

WHEN WE WALK ON HOB MOOR TODAY, we may hear the skylarks singing and we can appreciate the whole dome of the sky; we see a large open space, apparently very flat and featureless, with some housing at the boundaries but also considerable lengths of hedge, mostly of hawthorn. In winter, we see that the area is ill-drained in some parts. We can see the Minster at all seasons as it is situated on a higher part of York, and we may realise, if we approached from Tadcaster Road, that we came down an obvious slope. How does Hob Moor come to be as we know it today?

Towards the end of the last Ice Age, about 15000 years ago, a glacier perhaps almost a mile thick was advancing down the Vale of York from the north during the last major phase of glaciation. At its maximum extent, it reached as far south as the area where Wroot (east of Doncaster) now is. When the climate warmed and the ice retreated, it dumped a vast quantity of material which it had picked up on the way. Two prominent features it left behind were the two uneven ridges – the so-called York and Escrick moraines – which rose from an undulating landscape of bare sand and gravel banks spread over stiff clay containing boulders large and small. In some places, huge blocks of ice had broken off and were left to melt slowly as the main ice sheet continued its retreat. The resulting surface was characterised by depressions and general unevenness – and Hob Moor would eventually develop in one such large depression.

As can be seen from the sketch-map on the next page, Hob Moor is in the northern half of a shallow elongated bowl drained by Holgate Beck and Chaloners Whin Drain, together with a few small tributaries, and this catchment is almost entirely surrounded by higher land over 15m (50'). To the east and south is the ridge of the York moraine along which Tadcaster Road runs; to the north is Severus Hill; to the west is the higher land where Askham Bryan and Askham Richard are situated. After the retreat of the glacier for the last time (to date!), the bowl was much deeper but was subsequently infilled by lake clays, when much of the Vale of York became filled with a vast lake.

We know details of these deposits in the bowl because they were preserved in the clays which were dug extensively thousands of years later by the brickmakers of Dringhouses. The sketch-map shows the location of all the various claypits which were worked in the 19th and 20th centuries; the workers noticed that the clay they were digging was laminated – the layers representing sediment deposited in the lake-bottom each season – and that the laminations had been laid down over the uneven surface of the underlying glacial material.

At the south end of the bowl, upstream of Hob Moor, is Askham Bog. Much detailed work has been done on the sequence of deposits of this most important site and, through analysis of the pollen trapped in the various layers, we know the history of the post-glacial vegetation of the area. The desolate landscape of gravels, sands, clays and lakes was first colonised by herbs (including meadowsweet and sorrel), grasses, mosses, lichens and low-growing shrubs, but no trees. Climatic improvement allowed water plants to flourish and lime, oak, elm and hazel became established. About 7000 years ago, peat slowly began to accumulate and pollen from these layers suggests that alder was the most important tree species in the area nearby whilst the other forest trees continued to flourish further away.

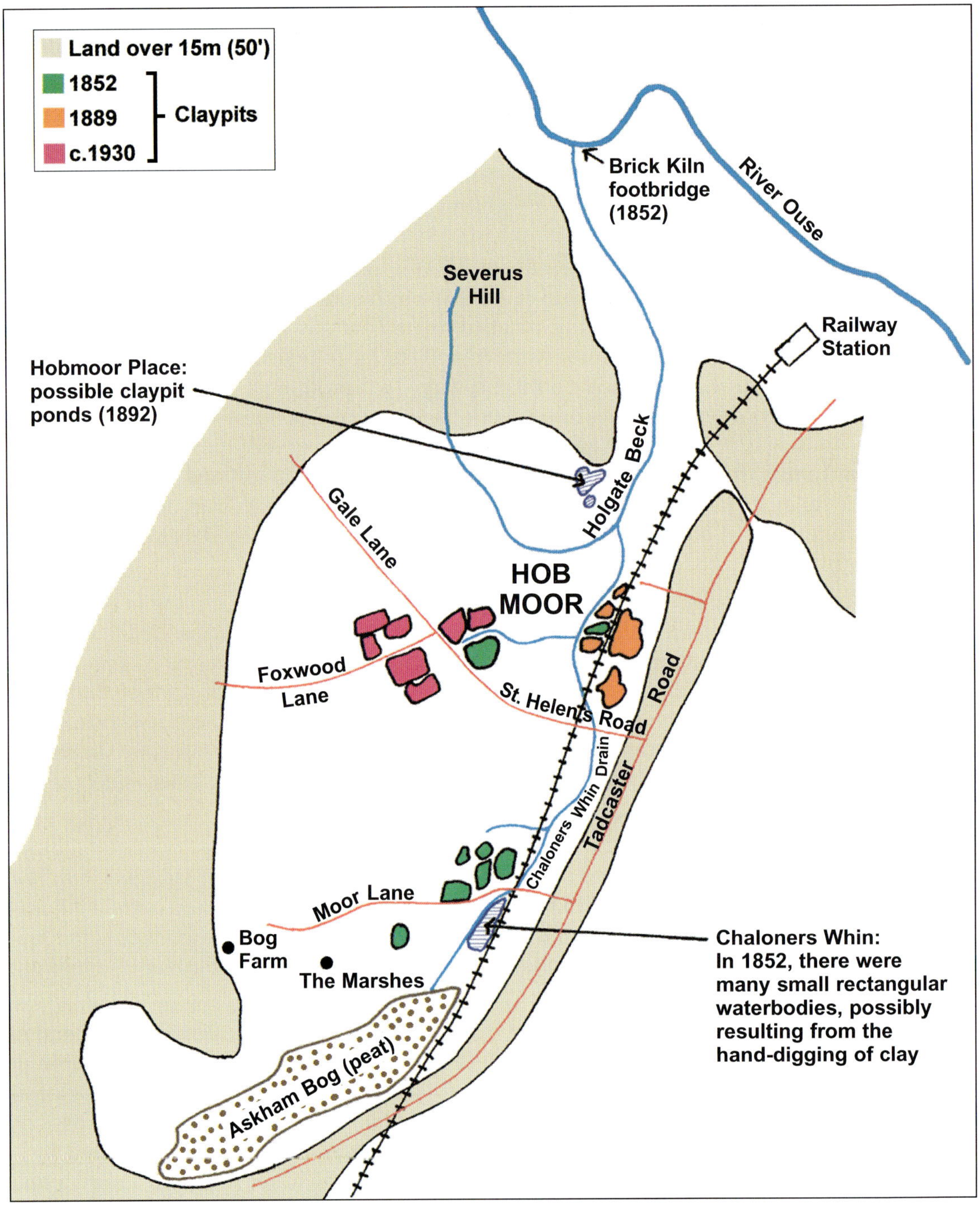

Sketch-map showing physical geography of catchment area and location of claypits.

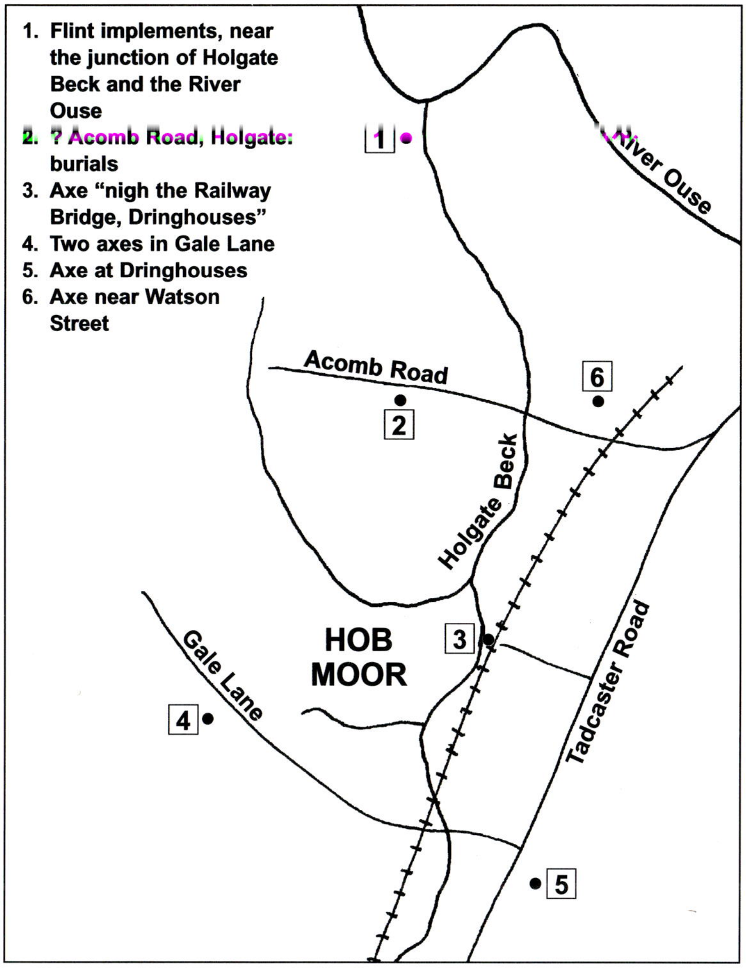

Evidence of Neolithic people: locations of finds.

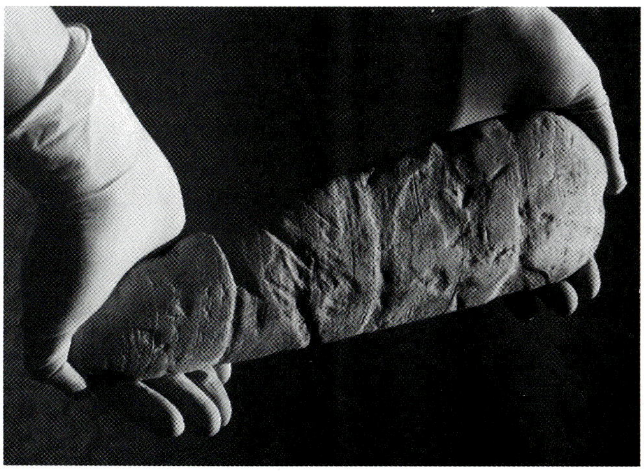

Neolithic axe found in 1999 in Watson Street. It is made of polished magnesian limestone, a material which is too soft for the axe to have been used as a tool. It would probably have been used for ritualistic purposes. Other evidence found suggests that there was perhaps prehistoric occupation of the site, or that it was perhaps a site where prehistoric peoples cast offerings to their gods. (Simon I Hill FRPS (Scirebroc) for York Archaeological Trust)

Peat has also been found on the site of the former Backhouse Nurseries and at St Paul's Square.

The larger animals, including woolly mammoth, which roamed around the north of England during the Glacial Period, did not return after the final retreat of the ice sheet, but reindeer, elk, giant deer and giant ox began to migrate, and lynx, brown bear and wolf were re-established. Over many centuries, the lakes were largely infilled with sediment and, by about 3000 BC, the virgin forest – the Wildwood – which had developed was just beginning to be affected by human activity. Early hunter-gatherers had already lived in North Yorkshire, as is evidenced by the camp site at Star Carr in the Vale of Pickering; here it has been established that the small settlement was at the lake edge and that there was a brushwood platform of axe-felled birch trees and branches which bridged the gap between the settlement and the open water of the lake. Perhaps there was a similar settlement at the edge of the lake, also bordered by reedbeds, at Askham Bog?

Clearings were created in the Wildwood as agricultural practices were introduced during the next thousand years by the Neolithic people. Most of the evidence for their presence in the York area has been found in the area to the south-west of the Ouse, and some of the most important items have been found near Hob Moor and Holgate Beck. A unique hoard of at least forty-three flint implements, including seven axes, was found in 1868 near the junction of Holgate Beck and the Ouse, and evidence of late Neolithic burials was found in Holgate, probably in Acomb Road. Other axes have been found: one "nigh the Railway Bridge, Dringhouses" in 1851 (this must refer to the railway underbridge between Hob Moor and Little Hob Moor as in 1851 there were no bridges across roads in Dringhouses – the 1852 Ordnance Survey map shows "North Lane Gate" and "Chaloner Whin Gate" at the two crossing points); two in Gale Lane; and one at Dringhouses. Most recently, a Neolithic axe was found in 1999 in a peat deposit in Watson Street.

Even though since Neolithic times the natural processes of erosion and the deposition of alluvium and wind-blown sand have of course resulted in the raising of the level of the land surface, we are quite justified in imagining our very early ancestors establishing hearth and home in the area around Hob Moor, exploiting the resources of lake and forest and developing early farming practices.

Post-glacial animals: mounted examples of wolf and brown bear kept at the Yorkshire Museum. (York Museums Trust (Yorkshire Museum))

2. The Romans

GIVEN THE AMOUNT OF EVIDENCE of the Roman occupation already found in the south west area of York, it is reasonable to assume that the Romans must have walked on Hob Moor.

Between about 2000 BC and the arrival of the Romans, we know that firstly Bronze Age and then Iron Age peoples were living in Yorkshire and that the ridge of higher land in the York area was used in an established network of major and minor communications. Indeed, it was part of a well-defined east-west trade route from Irish metal sources to East Yorkshire and the continent. This route was subsequently used also by the Romans as they travelled between Eboracum (York) and Calcaria (Tadcaster).

Short lengths of this Roman road have been found in Dringhouses, coinciding with the modern road as far north as the Methodist Chapel but between there and York diverging slightly from it to the west. Excavations on Little Hob Moor in 1954 and 1956, between the allotments and Hob Lane, revealed a Roman metalled surface about 37.5cm (15") below present ground level. It was assumed that this was part of the Roman road but its width was established as being 21m (67') and as yet this unusually wide surface (twice what might have been expected) has not been satisfactorily explained.

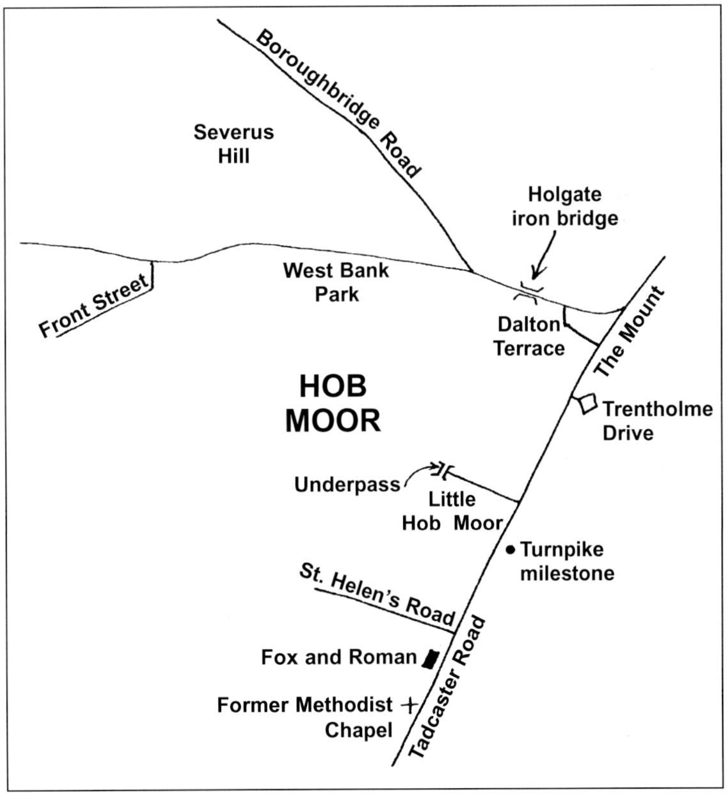

The Romans. Sketch-map showing locations of evidence mentioned in the text.

In addition to evidence of the Romans being found in the green area we now call Little Hob Moor, there is other important evidence of their presence in the wider area centred on Hob Moor itself.

In Dringhouses, evidence of a non-military, high-status Roman settlement, including fineware pottery, timber buildings and an iron-smelting furnace, has been found; also an area of burials around the junction of Tadcaster Road with St Helen's Road; an isolated burial just south of the turnpike milestone near the Knavesmire; and a small altar of white limestone just south of the erstwhile Fox Inn. Also found in Dringhouses was a fine tomb relief 48cm x 104cm x 16.5cm (1'7" x 3'5" x 6.5") of a smith.

In Acomb, behind a house in Front Street, a mosaic floor has been noted; stone coffins and Roman pottery were dug up in West Bank Park, the site being marked on the 1852 6" Ordnance Survey map; and a length of Roman Road has been located going over Severus Hill.

Roman burials, both of bodies and of ashes, have been found in large numbers in the areas of Dalton Terrace, The Mount School, Trentholme Drive, and The Mount. An isolated burial was found on the line of the railway, between the underpass and Holgate iron bridge.

The location of many of these burials reflects the Roman custom of burying their dead outside the settlements, along the main roads.

The area around York which the soldiers of the Ninth Legion found was already a cleared and cultivated landscape with patches of woodland, scrub and marsh. The hinterland of York must have been farmed by the Romans to produce cereals (especially wheat), and beef, lamb and pork. York became the most important Roman town in Northern Britain – and this population had to be fed and clothed. It is more than likely that the area of higher ground where Askham Bryan and Askham Richard are now sited was used for food production and that some villas were built in the vicinity. The principal roads to the south and west of Roman York were the present-day roads to Tadcaster and Boroughbridge. There was apparently no communications link coming into York through the wide area between these two. However, there is a Roman coffin, found in a nearby field, in the churchyard at Askham Richard, and the church at Askham Bryan contains some Roman tiles in the masonry.

Moreover, the 1852 map shows a footpath coming across the fields from Askham Richard and Askham Bryan, crossing Hob Moor and heading straight for the centre of York. York Minster is visible from many miles away; in Roman times, the landscape being little wooded, the Roman legionary headquarters, sited where the Minster now stands, would also presumably have been visible from a distance. The known Roman roads are only a small part of a communications system that was composed of main highways, lanes and causeways. Perhaps the causeway on Hob Moor has its origins as far back as Roman times when, avoiding the main roads used by the army, people took the shortest practicable route to reach Eboracum, bringing food and other goods. It could have joined up with a very short length of Roman road in the Dalton Terrace area, the existence of which has not yet been satisfactorily explained and where, as previously mentioned, many Roman burials have been found.

Tomb relief found at Dringhouses. The smith is holding an object on an anvil and is forging it with a hammer. (York Museums Trust (Yorkshire Museum))

The Roman coffin in the churchyard at Askham Richard.

3. Hob Moor – Ancient Stray

THE ORIGINS OF THE STRAYS (commons) of York and the way in which their management developed through the Middle Ages are shrouded in mystery. However, it would appear that soils, drainage (or the lack of it), and communications determined the use of Hob Moor as an area for grazing animals.

The nearby settlements of Acomb, Dringhouses and Holgate were all founded before the Norman Conquest, the first two on dry, higher land, and Holgate at the point where the present-day roads from Wetherby and Boroughbridge joined at the bridging point over Holgate Beck. The land nearer the villages was cultivated, leaving Hob Moor as a relatively ill-drained pasture.

Such ill-drained pastureland was certainly not without value. The right to pasture cattle and horses on common land in and around York became a jealously guarded privilege of the "freemen" of York, probably even in pre-Conquest times. These early freemen were landowners, ambitious, keen to improve their local status and increasingly influential. Their business was farming, and many will have lived on the outskirts of the city.

Today, cattle graze on Hob Moor from May until October. In some ways, such an arrangement is reminiscent of the pattern of medieval farming, for many of the extensive

Cattle on Hob Moor, May 2004. (I Tomlinson)

tracts of land reaching out of the city were used for pasturage during part of the year only. Then, it was the winter months that saw the cattle move in, as soon as the crops had been harvested. Historically, however, Hob Moor was common land, and therefore all-year pasture, part of the large area of rough, poorly drained land to the south of the city. Together with the Knavesmire, Hob Moor was used almost exclusively by the "pasturing freemen" (a term which distinguishes them from those later freemen who gained their positions from commerce). Only once in its history, during the Napoleonic Wars, has the ancient common of Hob Moor witnessed arable farming.

Rights of pasturage on the common land and on the strays of York were constantly being amended in the Middle Ages, partly because the number of freemen steadily increased, and frequently there were disputes. A stint, or share, was imposed, whereby each individual was allowed to graze a certain number of cattle and horses but, on Hob Moor, no sheep. It became customary for a freeman to graze his quota of stock on the stray attached to the ward in which he lived, under the care of the Pasture Masters. By 1624, Hob Moor was intercommoned (ie its use was shared) with Holgate, and the Knavesmire with Dringhouses and Middlethorpe.

Despite a series of enclosure acts between the 17th and 19th centuries, Hob Moor remained unenclosed and control of it remained with the freemen. Only in the 20th century was that control finally wrested – some would say illegally – from them, when, by an Act of Parliament passed in 1907, the ownership and management of Micklegate Stray (which includes Hob Moor) were taken over by the City Corporation.

In the York City Archives, there are twelve documents containing accounts of the riding of the city boundaries, the first of which dates from 1374 and is in one of the earliest records of municipal matters in York, the first Memorandum Book. The description includes "yhorkesmore" as the name for the present-day Hob Moor; "Yorks Moor" continued to be used until 1802 when the area was referred to as "what was Yorks Moor". However, Hob Moor, Obmore and Hobb Moor were also used in other documents. Presumably, in earlier times, it was important to emphasise that this particular pasture belonged to the City of York, since it was almost surrounded by land that did <u>not</u> so belong. It should be borne in mind that Holgate became part of York only in 1884 and Acomb and Dringhouses even later, after a further extension of the municipal boundaries in 1937.

In "riding the bounds", the mayor and his party were riding round the land over which the citizens enjoyed rights of pasturage and those rights were thereby confirmed. In 1500, several members of the mayor's following protested that the boundary they had ridden between the Knavesmire and Yorkesmore had exceeded the limits of the City of York, and this is noted in the margin of the document. Other documents tend to give a confusing picture, due to the fields adjacent to Yorks Moor being given different names at different times.

In spite of all this, however, the boundary descriptions are in accord that the line of the city boundary went right round Hob Moor, including it in the city, and this is confirmed several centuries later by the 1852 6" Ordnance Survey map. Boundary stones are marked at frequent intervals along its length, usually at a change of direction; sadly, none of those marked on Hob Moor is still visible but two on the Knavesmire can still be seen, at the corner opposite Ainsty Grove and at the bottom of the slope running down from there, as can the one beside Tadcaster Road, opposite the end of Hob Lane.

Boundary stone on the Knavesmire.

Boundary stone opposite the end of Hob Lane.

The former streamline at the western edge of the Ancient Stray.

The boundary of Hob Moor was unchanged for centuries until some areas adjacent to the Ancient Stray were added, resulting in the large open space of irregular outline which we now know as Hob Moor. It can be seen from the 1852 map that the boundary was formed by streams, even along the western edge where a direction-of-flow arrow shows that this particular stream was flowing south. The line of this former stream is still visible as a wiggly depression, water-filled after wet weather.

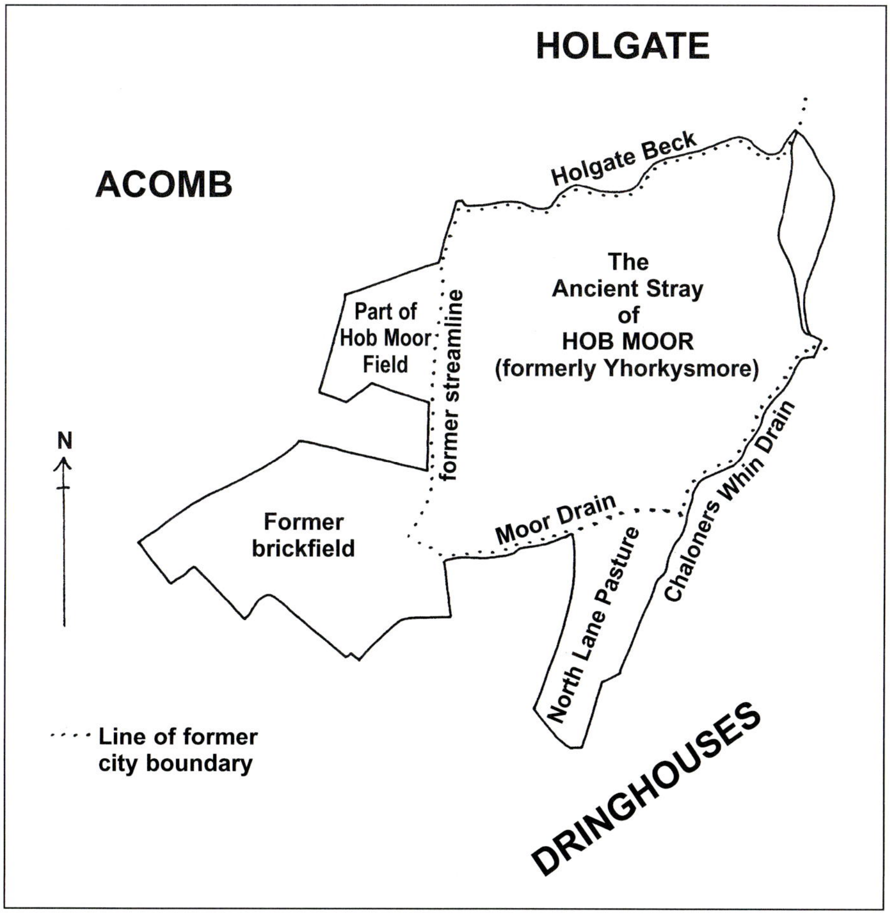

Hob Moor as it is today, showing its component parts.

4. The Water-mill and the Two-Acre Close

IN MEDIEVAL TIMES, there were in the vicinity of York several windmills and three water-mills. Of the latter, one stood in the north-east corner of Hob Moor. The first documentary reference to it, in 1563, is in an agreement by the City that Robert Deighton, mylner (miller), should have a twenty-one-year lease of the "mylne called Hobmylne and a closse ... conteyning by estymacon twoo acres of land." From 1581 onwards, it is referred to as Folly Mylne and the bridge nearby as Folly Mylne Brigg, but the close was referred to as "Hob Mill Close" when it was let in 1723, without the mill, "the house being down". It may be that the name "Folly" is a corruption of "Fulling", in which case the water-mill may have been used for fulling, ie cleansing and thickening cloth, but in 1605 it was in use for the grinding of corn.

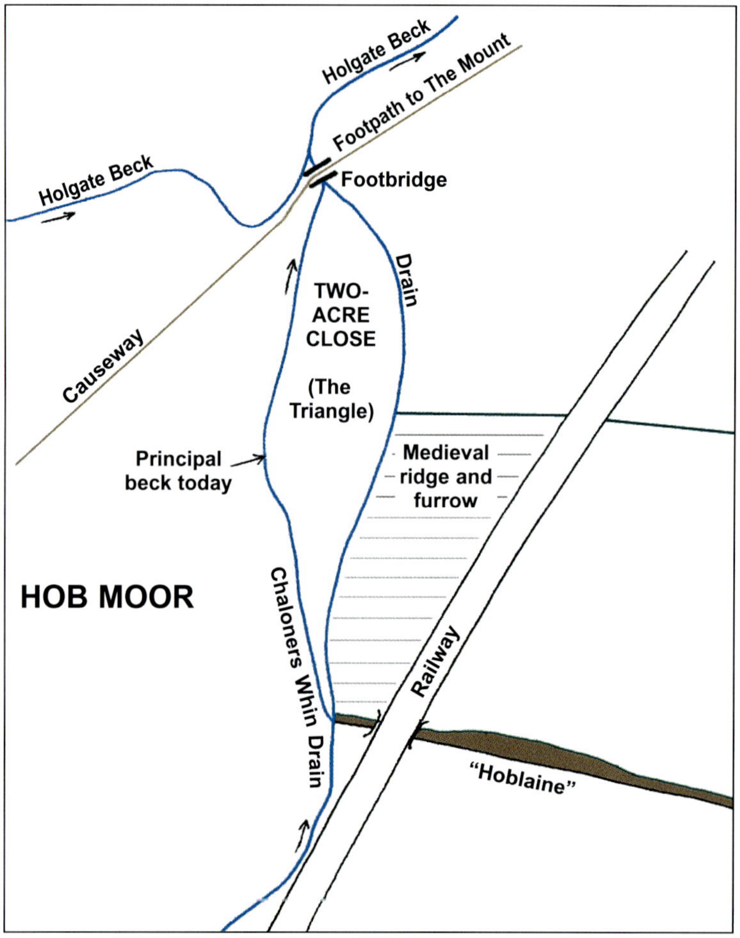

The north-east corner of Hob Moor (base map: 1892 25" Ordnance Survey map).

The exact location of Folly Mill is, at the time of writing, a mystery. However, it seems reasonable to make several assumptions:

- The Two-Acre Close, which was always let by the City in close association with the water-mill, must be the area which we call The Triangle. This area is clearly marked as being "On City Land" on the 1729 map of Bishop Fields and is the "island" between the present-day beck and a drain to the east (see sketch-map).
- The beck, now called Chaloners Whin Drain, along the whole of the eastern side of Hob Moor drains a large area including Askham Bog and in medieval times was most probably carrying a greater flow than Holgate Beck. The present rates of flow cannot usefully be taken as indicators, due to changes to the drainage basin since the 1960s, but as recently as the 1950s Chaloners Whin Drain was a much bigger stream than Holgate Beck. In Drake's *Eboracum* (1736), a map clearly shows the stream draining out of the Bog, whereas Holgate Beck and other tributaries are not important enough to be shown.
- An aerial photograph taken in 1936, when Hob Moor was used as a golf course, shows medieval ridge and furrow in the field immediately to the east of the Two-Acre Close, but stopping at the small drain. Furthermore, detailed study of this corner of Hob Moor shows that the drain is at the bottom of the natural slope. The drain was thus the natural beck and what is today the principal beck along the western edge of The Triangle was cut at some stage, possibly as a drainage channel, thereby creating the Two-Acre Close.
- A document of 1602 refers to access to the mill being via "Hoblaine", the lane leading down from Tadcaster Road. There does not appear to have been a significant approach from Holgate; presumably the large field north of Hob Moor was called Folly Mill Field because it was the field nearest to the mill and not because the mill was sited at the edge of it. Moreover, a document of 1605 refers to "a close and watter mill on Yorke moor"; for centuries, Hob Moor was called Yorke (or Yorks) Moor.

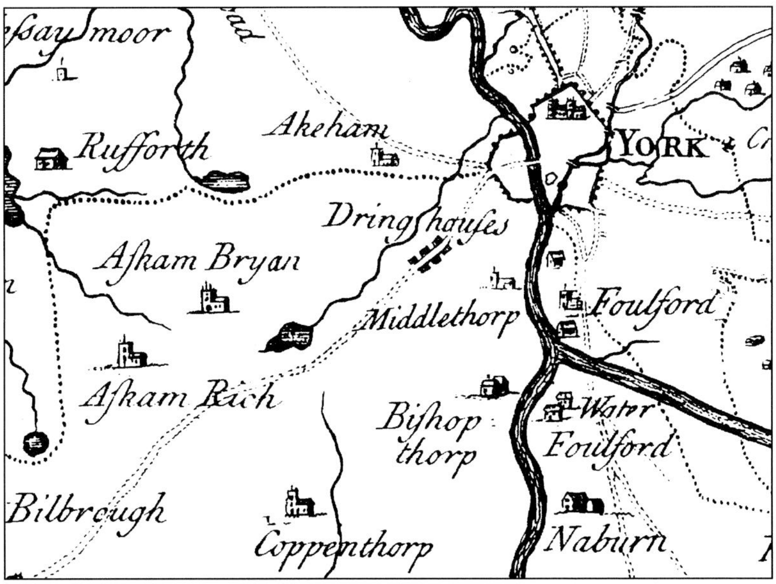

Part of Francis Drake's map of "York, its boundarys, the peculiar districk, Aynsty, belonging to it;...with a draught of the grand project for cutting a Canal from the Humber to the City, anno 1616." (York City Archives)

Aerial photograph of 1936. (York City Archives)

The principal stream along the western edge of The Triangle, looking north. Until the 1990s, this stream had higher, steeper banks; then this broad access path was created by removing up to 1m (3') of soil which was dumped to form an elongated mound immediately to the right of the path.

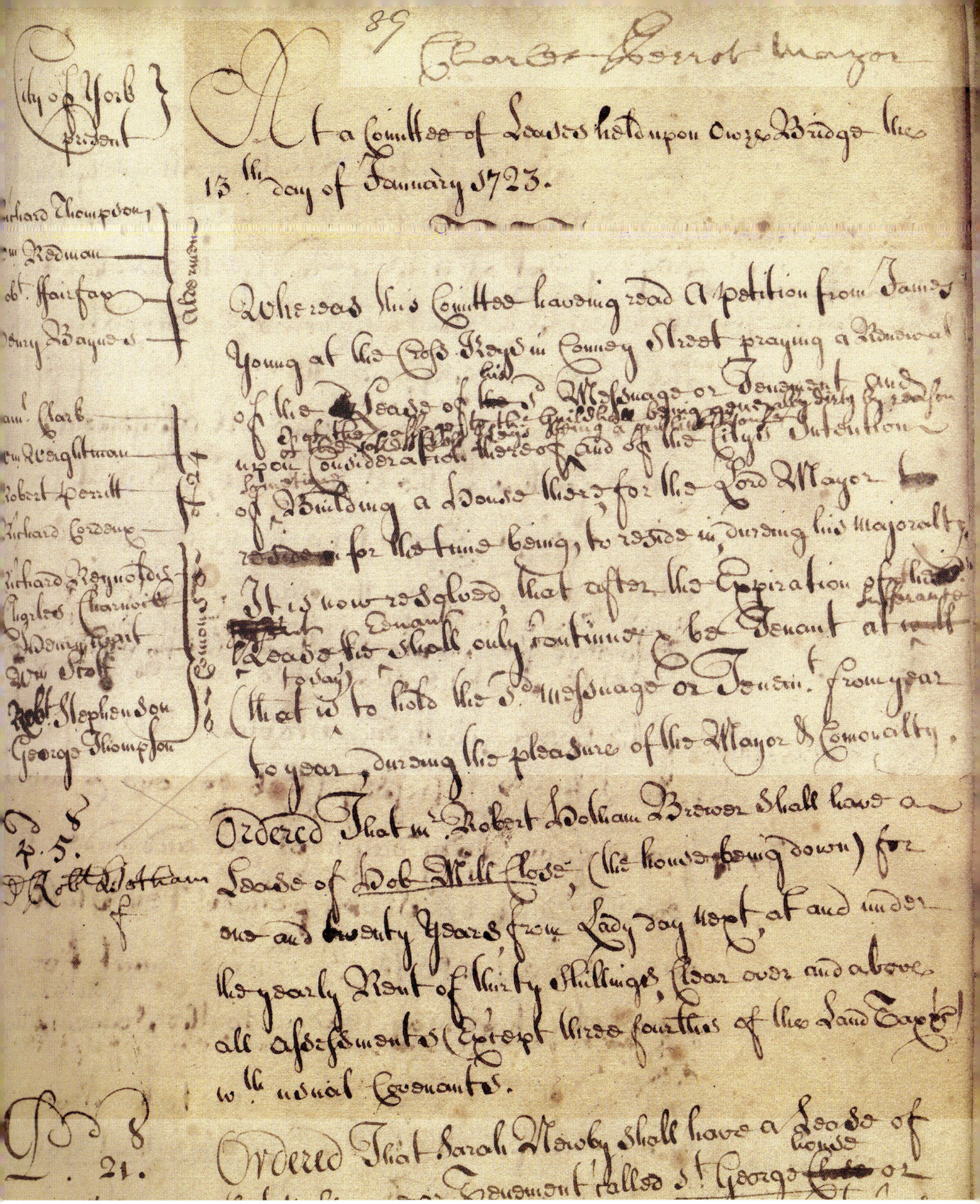
89 Charles Perrot Mayor

City of York } President

Richard Thompson
Wm Redman
Robt. Fairfax
Henry Baynes
Aldermen

Saml. Clark
Wm Wrightman
Robert Perritt
Richard Cordeux
Richard Reynolds
Charles Charnock
[illegible]
Wm Stoff
Robt. Stephenson
George Thompson
24
Commons

At a Comittee of Leases held upon Ouze Bridge the 13th day of January 1723.

Whereas this Comittee having read a petition from James Young at the Cross Keys in Conney Street praying a Renewal of the Lease of his sd Messuage or Tenement and [illegible] upon Consideration thereof and of the City's Intention of Building a House there for the Lord Mayor for the time being, to reside in, during his Mayoralty.

It is now resolved, that after the Expiration of the [illegible] Lease the Tenant Shall only continue to be Tenant at will (that is to say to hold the sd Messuage or Tenemt. from year to year, during the pleasure of the Mayor & Comonalty.

Ordered That Mr Robert Hotham Brewer Shall have a Lease of Hob Mill Close (the house being down) for one and twenty years from Lady day next, at and under the yearly Rent of thirty Shillings, Clear over and above all Assessments (Except three fourths of the Land Tax) wth usual Covenants.

Ordered That Sarah Mawby Shall have a Lease of house [illegible] Tenement called St George [illegible]

The lease of Hob Mill Close to Robert Hotham, 1723 (York City Archives, E101/89): "Ordered That Mr Robert Hotham Brewer Shall have a lease of Hob Mill Close (the house being down) for one and twenty years from Lady day next at and under the yearly rent of thirty shillings Clear over and above all assessments (except three fourths of the Land Tax xs) with usual Covenants".

The main streams around Hob Moor have been much over-deepened in recent times, which impedes a good understanding of what they were like four hundred and more years ago. We await a geophysical survey of the area in order to see whether any evidence of the water-mill remains and if there is any trace of the existence of a millpond. A millpond was not necessarily a feature of all mill sites and it may well be that Askham Bog provided a steady flow of water to the mill all the year round, thus obviating the need for a pond.

Records show that the Two-Acre Close continued to be let, as Hob Mill Close. Some of the lessees were: Robert Hotham, brewer, in 1723; Matthew Wharton, wine cooper, in 1741; Thomas Speight in 1763; and in 1807, Joseph Wood, cutler. By this time it was known as the Cherry Orchard, a name which was used again on the Dringhouses Inclosure map of 1822. In January 1826, the Warden and Pasture Masters of Micklegate Ward ordered that £420 be offered for Cherry Orchard and later the same month the City ordered that it be sold and conveyed in trust for the Freemen and annexed to Hob Moor.

The water-mill, from the Luttrell Psalter. The Luttrell Psalter was written and illuminated in England circa 1335 for Sir Geoffrey Luttrell of Irnham in Lincolnshire: scenes of everyday life and religious images surround the texts. This illustration shows a water-mill, timber-framed and with a thatched roof, the mill wheel, and the mill leat with fish traps already successful here in catching a fish and an eel. To harness the power of streams which had only negligible fall, the mill wheel could be placed horizontally, or could be undershot (not overshot, as in this illustration). (By permission of The British Library; Add. 42130 f181)

5. *John and Anne Overend, Millers*

AROUND THE YEAR 1600, spelling was not consistent, and the hearing of those responsible for the writing of documents was perhaps not always adequate to the task! Thus the surname of John and Anne appears in different guises: Overend, Overinge, Hoverynge, Overyn and Overen. Because of the content of the documents, it can be said with certainty that only one John and Anne Overend are involved; in order to preserve as much as possible of the authenticity and integrity of the documents, the spelling used in each case will be reproduced here.

The first reference to John Overend is in a document (folio 210 in House Book 32, York City Archives) dated 18 June 1602, when he was granted by the City a new lease of Folly Mill and Close. It had previously been agreed in November 1600 that:

> folly milne then late burnt by some unbeknowne person whereof John overend was tenant That the same shold be newly builded by the tenant who craved a new lease thereof And That after the newe buildinge thereof that the same shold be vewed.

In June 1602, Andrew Trewe, Henry Hall, Thomas Harbert, Alderman, and Robert Harryson, Sheriff, having viewed Folly Milne, considered that the tenant had "bestowed great cost in the new buildinge of the same mylne and that he shold have a newe lease therof frome Pentecost Last", for twenty-five years. John was required to "sufficiently repair and maintayn the same duringe the said tearme"; the City undertook to repair a stone bridge and a wooden bridge and the "cawsey" (track) called "Hoblaine" leading to "Hobmore" and to the mill; after this work, John was to be responsible for their maintenance.

As a miller, John Overend would have been an important and skilful member of his local community, responsible for grinding the corn brought to him from the surrounding area and thus having a crucial role in the production of bread. In addition to overseeing the grinding of the corn brought by each customer, a miller had to see to the sluices and regulate the water flow; keep the wheels in good repair by replacing worn paddles and cogs; maintain the sharp edges of the furrows on the faces of the stones; make sure that the shape of the stones directed the meal towards the periphery; regulate the speed of the stones and the gap between them, and the rate at which the grain was fed to them. The miller was thus required to manhandle not only the sacks of grain but also the millstones when he needed to work on them. A working water-mill, together with examples of millstones with different patterns of furrows, can be seen at York Castle Museum where the old Raindale Mill has been reconstructed beside the River Foss.

Having been granted a twenty-five-year lease, John and Anne Overend must have looked forward to a period of relative stability. However, in the registers of St Mary Bishophill Junior there is recorded:

> Buriall: John Hoverynge was buried the xiiii day of november in the 2 year of King James 1604.

The burial of Katren Hoverynge had already been recorded on 16 September 1604 and she may have been John and Anne's daughter as, in his will, John asked to be buried "in the Churchyard of Bishophill the younger set nere my daughter as may be".

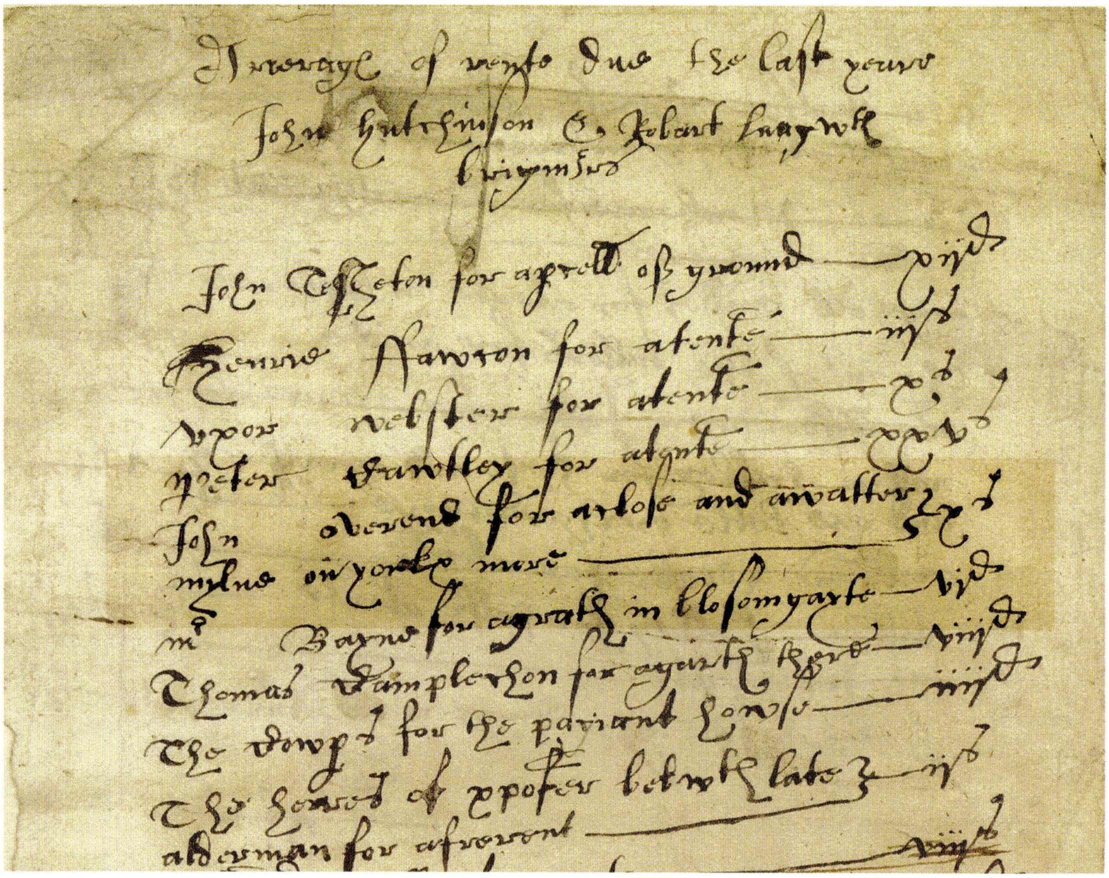

Arrerage of rents due the last yeare
John Hutchinson & Robert [illegible]
Chamberlins

John [illegible] for a grownd [illegible]
Henrie [illegible] for a tente iijs
[illegible] webster for a tente xs
Peter [illegible] for a tente xxs
John Overend for a close and a watter mylne on yorke more xs
Mr [illegible] for a garth in Blossomgate vjd
Thomas [illegible] for a garth [illegible]
The [illegible] for the pagiant howse iiijs
The howse of [illegible] iijs
[illegible] for a [illegible]

John Overend's arrears. (York City Archives, CB12/178)

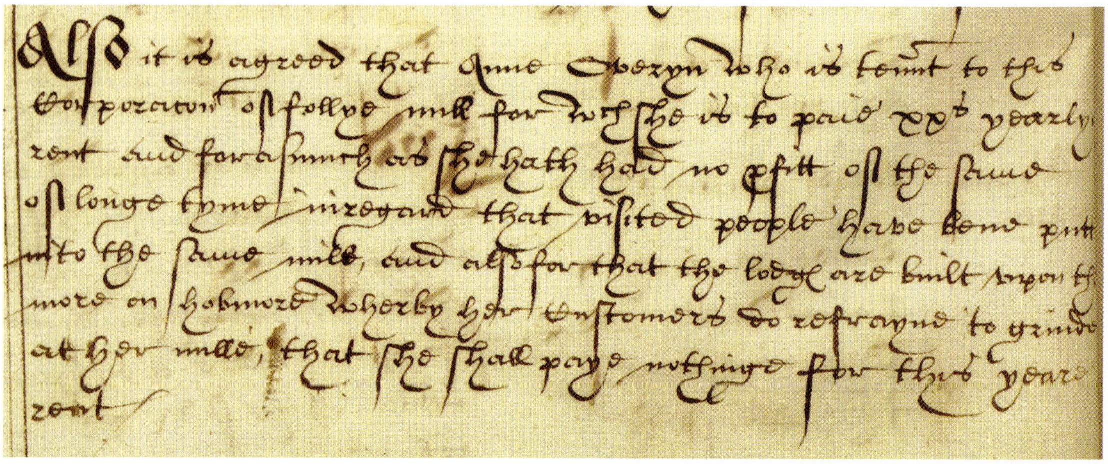

Also it is agreed that Anne Overyn who is tenant to this Corporacion of Follye mill for which she is to paie xxs yearly rent and forasmuch as she hath had no profitt of the same of longe tyme in regard that visited people have bene putt into the same mill, and also for that the lodges are built upon the more on Hobmore wherby her Customers do refrayne to grinde at her mill, that she shall paye nothinge for this yeare rent

Anne Overyn is excused payment of rent for Folly Mill due to plague victims having been housed there. (York City Archives, B32/359v)

John's will begins in the fashion customary at the time:

> In the name of God, Amen. The ixth day of November, 1604. I John Overen of the Suburbes of the Cytty of yorke Milner of the parishe of Bishophill the younger beinge sick in body but whole in mynde and memory I do ordeyne and make this my last will and testament in manner and forme following.

He leaves his land and house to his wife, and the residue of his estate, after other bequests and burial and funeral expenses, to his wife and to his son Thomas. Anne Overend, widow of the deceased, was the sole executrix; probate was granted on 26 February 1605, for the will of John Overen, milner.

An entry in the Chamberlain's Accounts for 1605, but pertaining to 1604, confirms that disaster struck the Overend family, as John is noted as owing rent arrears of ten shillings "for a close and watter mylne on Yorke moor". The arrears were recorded in the year following that in which they were incurred and it was not mentioned that the tenant was deceased.

Another document indicates that Anne took over the tenancy after her husband's death. It was recorded on 29 May 1605:

> Also it is agreed that Anne Overyn who is tenant to this corporation of follye mill for which she is to paie XXs yearlye rent and forasmuch she hath had no profitt of the same of longe tyme in regard that visited people have bene putt into the same mill, and also that the lodges are built upon the more on Hobmore wherby her customers do refrayne to grinde at her mill that she shall paye nothinge for this yeare rent.

Anne subsequently married one Nicholas Dannyell. The event is recorded in the same registers mentioned above:

> Nicholas Danyell and Anne Overinge widow tuesday the xith June 1605

They must have lived in Dringhouses. Nicholas Dannyell's name is in the list of jury of the Manor of Dringhouses in a document, dated 22 October 1639, giving details of paines (fines) imposed on villagers for various misdeeds. Anne died in 1630, her burial being recorded in the same registers:

> Anne Danniell of Ringhouses xiith day of September 1630

Having survived the plague which had (presumably) caused the death of her first husband, she had outlived him by nearly twenty-six years.

The tower of St Mary Bishophill Junior. The pre-Conquest tower and much of the interior of this church are unchanged since 1600.

6. *Hob Moor: Place of Exile*

THE 1604 OUTBREAK OF PLAGUE in York was not the first time that York had suffered or that Hob Moor had been envisaged as a suitable place for housing some of the victims. The Civic Records tell us that already in 1549–50 money was set aside for the building of two lodges on Hob Moor for plague victims, in order to safeguard the city. There was a further outbreak in 1558–9 but there is no record of Hob Moor being used on that occasion. There then followed a period of over forty years without major threats to the health of York's citizens.

The great plague of 1604 had taken hold by the end of April in spite of watch having been kept to prevent infected persons and goods from entering the walls. Bubonic plague, spread when a flea bites its rodent host and then regurgitates its blood-meal into its next (human) host, is characterised by extremely painful swellings on the neck and in the armpits and groin. Whole households could be wiped out whilst others escaped unscathed. This particular outbreak killed over 3500 of York's citizens, almost a third of the city's population. The York plague-lodges were set up in three locations: in the Horsefair (Gillygate), at Clementhorpe, and on Hob Moor.

Some understanding of what happened on Hob Moor can be gained from a passage in the biography of Thomas Morton, written in 1669 by R Baddily, his Secretary. Thomas Morton, born in York in 1564, the sixth child of nineteen, was an extraordinary man.

In about 1597 he became Pastor of Long Marston near York, where "he spent his time in the diligent Preaching of Gods Word, unto the Parishioners there, and sometimes in other neighbouring places, especially where they most stood in need of Spirituall comfort and instruction."

Having spent some time in Cambridge and abroad, he was again at Long Marston during "that great and funebrious sickness of the Plague at York, whereof some thousands dyed; but the poorer sort of the infected were turned out of the City and had Booths Erected on Hob Moor, neer unto the City; For whose comfort and reliefe, in that fatall extremity, Mr Morton often repaired unto them from Marston to preach unto them the Word of God, and to Minister consolation to their languishing soules; having withall provisions of meat carried with him in Sacks, to relieve the poorest sort withall."

After a long career which saw him moving amongst the nobility, those in high office in the Church, and the poor, he was made Bishop of Durham in 1633. He was much travelled and a noted scholar, publishing tracts on the important religious issues of his time. Despite moving amongst the rich and influential, he lived very humbly. As Baddily writes: "As his Revenues increased, so were they expended in Hospitable, Charitable and other Christian uses." He died aged ninety-five.

As well as the plague-lodges, Folly Mill, in the north-east corner of Hob Moor, was used for housing plague victims. The principal access to the mill was down the slope from Tadcaster Road along "Hoblaine", so it seems reasonable to assume that this was the lane down which Thomas Morton rode, especially as it is beside this lane that the Plague Stone is located, on Little Hob Moor.

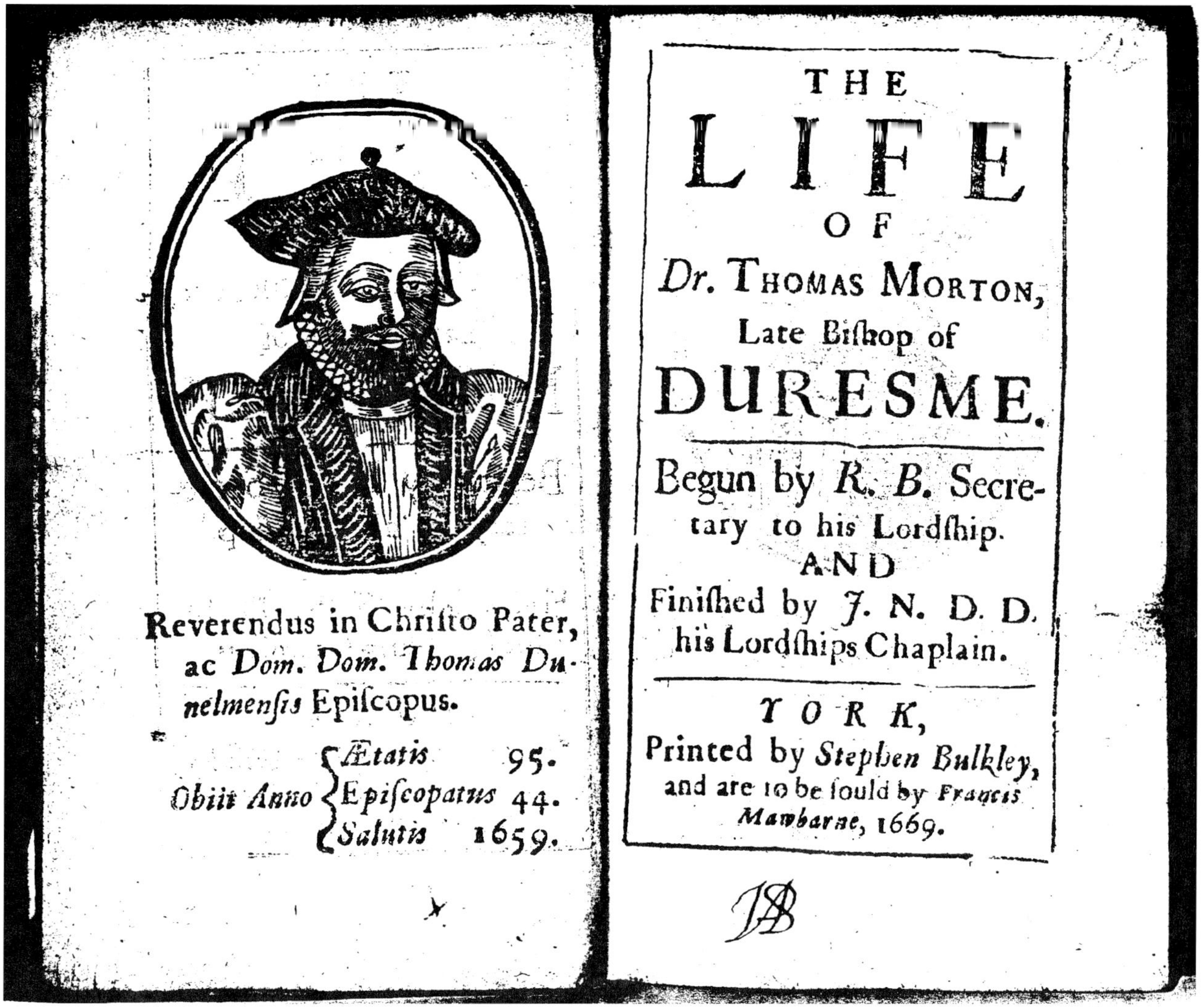

Reverendus in Chriſto Pater, ac Dom. Dom. Thomas Dunelmenſis Epiſcopus.

Obiit Anno { Ætatis 95. / Epiſcopatus 44. / Salutis 1659.

THE
LIFE
OF
Dr. THOMAS MORTON,
Late Biſhop of
DURESME.

Begun by R. B. Secretary to his Lordſhip.
AND
Finiſhed by J. N. D. D. his Lordſhips Chaplain.

YORK,
Printed by Stephen Bulkley, and are to be ſould by Francis Mawbarne, 1669.

Frontispiece and title page of R Baddily's biography of Thomas Morton (actual size).
(© Dean and Chapter of York: reproduced by kind permission)

The Plague Stone was discovered buried in the ground a short distance from its present position. It measures 63cm x 56cm (25" x 22"), with a shallow basin in the centre; it seems highly likely that money to pay for food brought out from the city was placed here, in water or vinegar as a disinfectant, by plague victims or those looking after them. At the instigation of The Gild of Freemen, the stone was cleaned and restored in 1988.

Whereabouts on Hob Moor were the plague lodges erected? For several reasons, they were most probably built in the north-east corner, on the Two-Acre Close:

– it belonged to the City
– it was remote from the rest of the population

The Plague Stone, Little Hob Moor.

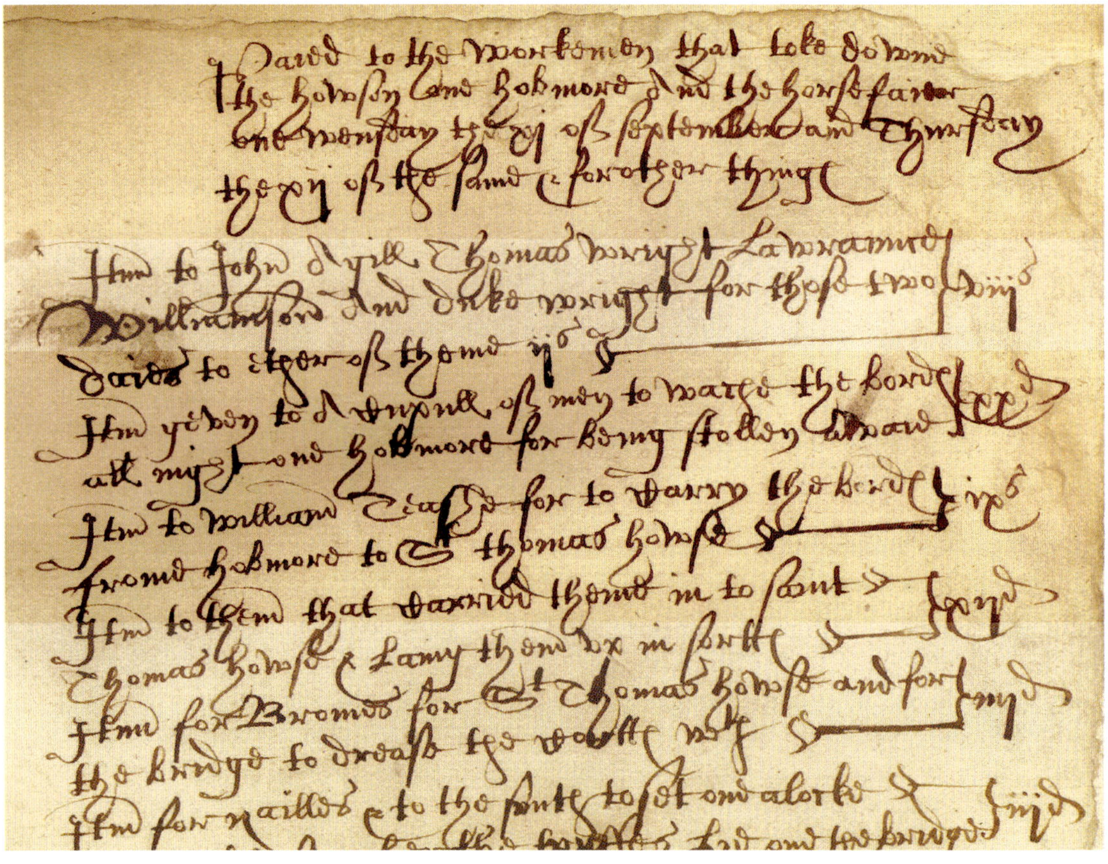

Part of the City of York Accounts, 1605 (York City Archives, CB12/165):
"Paid to the workemen that toke downe the howson one hobmore And the horsefair on wensday the xj September and Thursday the xij of the same and for other thinges"
"Item geven to a cupull of men to watch the bordes at night one hobmore for being stollen awaie xxd Item to William Teashe for to carry the bordes frome hobmore to St Thomas House ixs"

– it was an area bounded by streams and could thus be more easily isolated

– it had only one main access (via Hoblaine) so that comings and goings could be controlled.

By the time plague victims, perhaps with other family members, had been carried in great pain almost a mile out of town from Micklegate Bar and then even further away from all habitation down Hoblaine and into a remote corner of a large common, they must have felt truly exiled and hopeless. Thomas Morton's visits would have been immeasurably appreciated.

It is not possible to know how many victims were taken to Hob Moor, nor how many died and were buried there: on account of the large numbers of people dying, many burials remained unrecorded. However, the burial register of St Margaret's, York, contains the names of eight people who are recorded as having died of the plague on Hob Moor and as having been buried there:

Matthew Staynton on about 3 July 1604
Effania, his daughter, on about 6 July
Robert Greenwood on 1 August
Robert Watson on 11 August
Thomas, son of the above, on 11 August
William Wardle on 12 August
Alice Wardle, wife of William, on 15 August
Christopher Tomlinson on 17 August

We do not know whereabouts on Hob Moor these burials took place but clearly someone cared enough about these parishioners of St Margaret's to record their burial in the register.

When the "great and funebrious sickness" abated in the following summer, the plague lodges were removed. Details are given in the City's Accounts of the sums paid to those who kept a watch-out for thieves and to those who removed the "boards".

Thus ended the most harrowing period in the history of the City of York and the most harrowing event on Hob Moor.

7. Samuel Parsons' Map of Dringhouses, 1624

SAMUEL PARSONS WAS A SURVEYOR of national repute, working between 1618 and 1639 in Middlesex, Essex, Berkshire and Shropshire as well as in York. His map of Dringhouses, which includes parts of Hob Moor, is the earliest surviving large-scale plan of any part of York or its near neighbourhood and is of noteworthy accuracy.

This wonderful map, in colour and with the names still legible, shows the ownership of land in the Manor of Dringhouses. The inscription in the top left-hand corner reads:

> *The Plott of the Mannor of Dringhouses lyinge within the Countie of the Cittie of York.* Taken Anno Domini 1624 and made up 1629 by Samuell Parsons, survaier.

The map measures approximately 100cm x 66cm (38" x 26") and is in the City of York Reference Library.

The map, reproduced on pages 26-7, has south at the top. Thus, the Knavesmire is shown on the left-hand side of the road ("London Roade") to Tadcaster. On the right-hand side of this road, in the top half of the map, are written about a hundred and fifty individual names, each being that of the owner of that particular cultivated strip.

The enlargement on page 28 shows the lower right-hand part of Parsons' map. Hobb Lane is named, together with North Lane and Hobb Moore (Common to Yorke and Houlgate). The names of the owners of the individual strips in the fields at the southern end of Hob Moor are written along the alignment which we still see today in the ridges and furrows. The names of those who cultivated the strips in the field called Hobmoor Side furlong, part of which is now North Lane Pasture, include Raphe Naggs, Margeret Knaggs, Geo Allyn, A Breary, Tho Donnington, Mr Padmore and Wm Richmond.

The strips of each farmer were distributed either regularly or randomly around the village. All the strips were grouped into convenient blocks (called furlongs) within a field, and hedges were few, in order to allow communal work and the pasturing of an area in fallow years. The same crop was grown by all the farmers on any one furlong.

The aerial photograph on page 29, taken in 1936, shows the still unchanged southern boundary of the ancient common (then in use as a golf course) and the fields adjacent. The field strips can be seen, those in the smaller field (now The Pastures estate) at right angles to those in the larger field – as marked by Samuel Parsons on his map.

The ridge and furrow seen in North Lane Pasture is a particularly well-developed and excellently preserved example of this historic landscape feature. It was created over the centuries by ox-ploughing and has the characteristic reversed-S curvature of medieval ridge and furrow. The undulations will have ensured that there were ridges of better-drained soil, and it is noticeable on Parsons' map that the strips are at right angles to the nearest stream, thus facilitating drainage.

It will be seen on Parsons' map that the area now known as Little Hob Moor is divided into closes belonging to Alderman Breary and Mrs Weddall and that there is a house on Hobb Lane. Later, the St Mary Bishophill Junior register records the baptism of two children,

George and Jane, in 1666 and 1670/1 respectively, the son and daughter of William Brown of Hoblane.

Ox-ploughing, from the Luttrell Psalter (circa 1335). (By permission of The British Library; Add. 42130 f170)

North Lane Pasture, looking north. Ridge and furrow, the boundary hedge and the ancient common beyond.

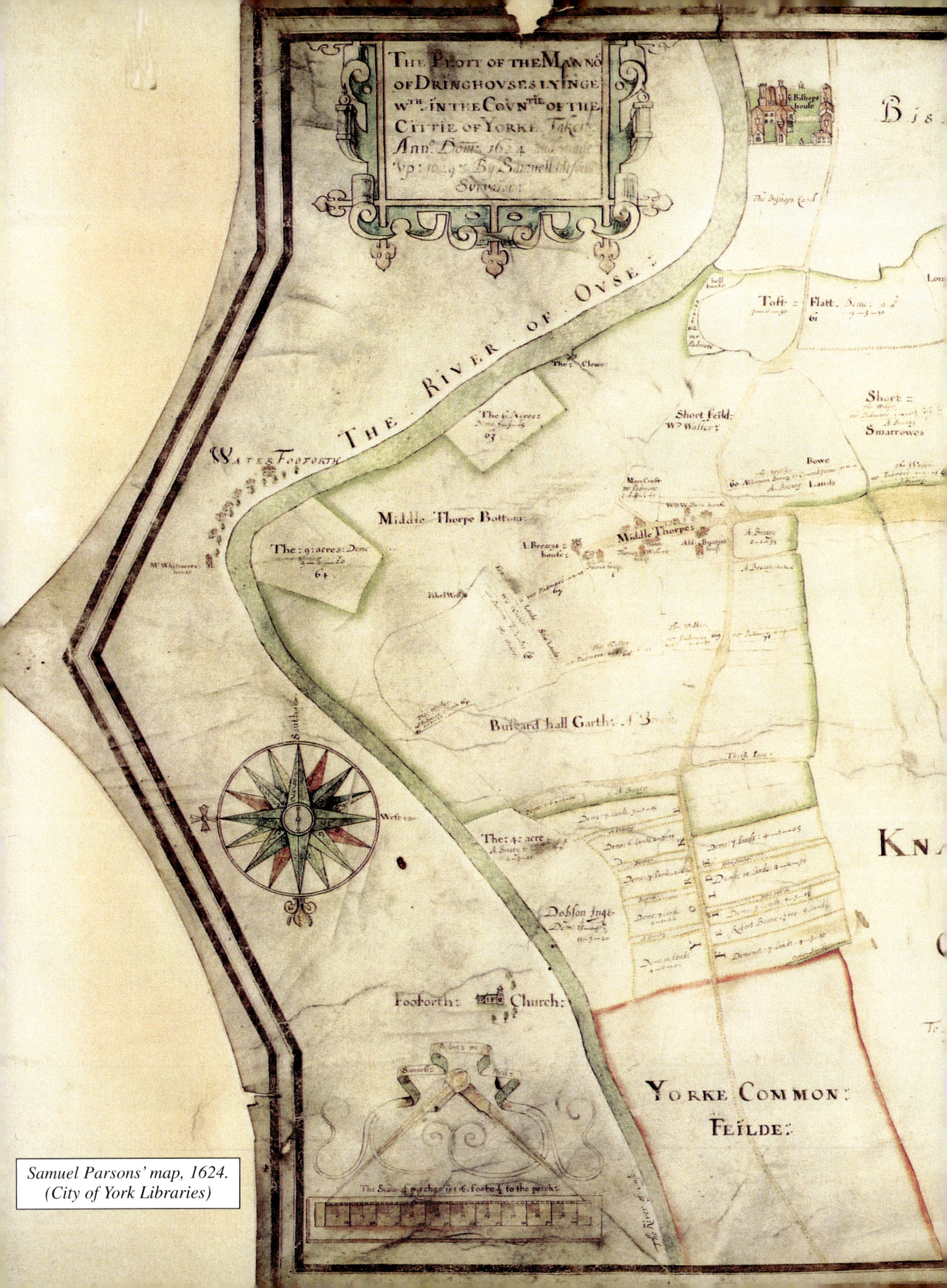

Samuel Parsons' map, 1624. (City of York Libraries)

Coppenthorpe Lord:pp
Thorpe Lordpp
Middle Thorpe Comõn Moore
New Enclosed
The Moore Landes
hougerhills
Alderman Breary
Streate Landes
Lone Roade
Dringhouses Common Moore
153—3—00
Acombe Lordshipp
The West Feilde
Dykecome Nooke
The Garth ends
The Intack
hall Close
Keyes Farme
Lane Close
Dringhouses
The Chappell Close
The North Feilde
ES MYRE
MMON
Middle Thorpe
Parts of Yorke
The Flatts
Mrs Weddell Freehould
Hobb Lane Close
Hobb Moore
Common to Yorke and Houget
Staines Close
Acombe hobb More
Acombe Lordship

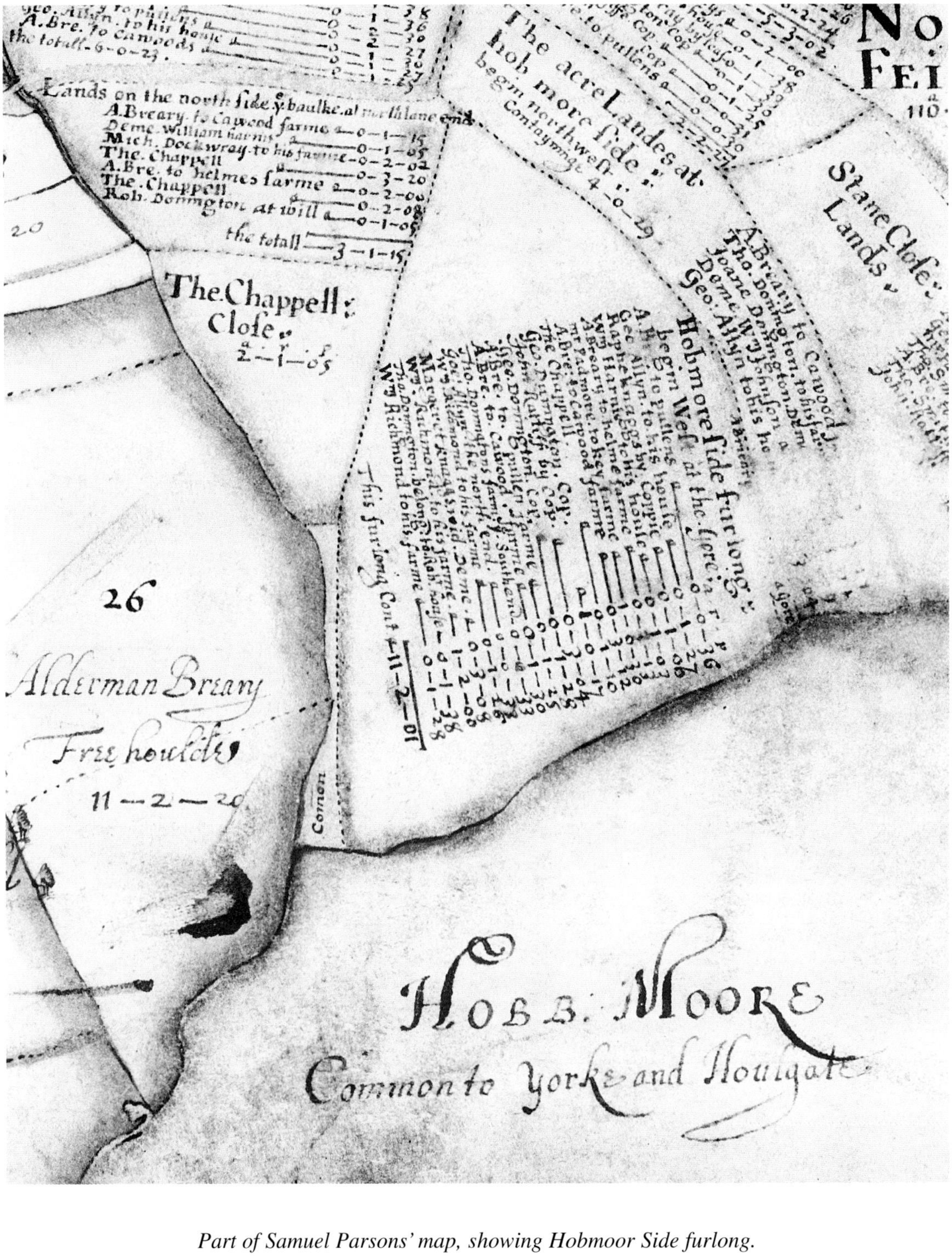

Part of Samuel Parsons' map, showing Hobmoor Side furlong.

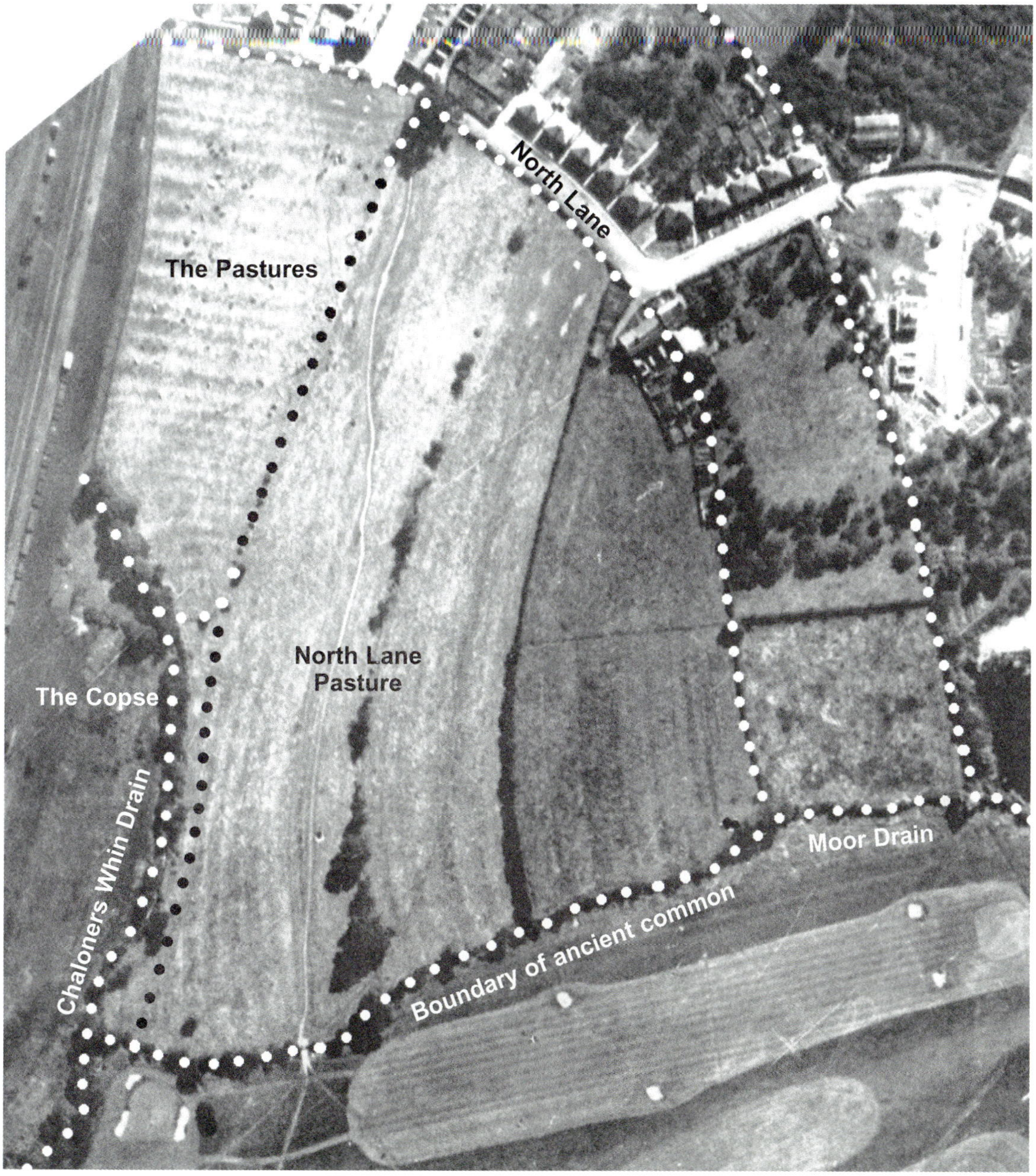

Aerial photograph of 1936, with the 1624 field boundaries indicated and present-day features named. (York City Archives)

A document in the Yorkshire Archaeological Society's archives, entitled "Paines imposed upon and by-lawes made by the tenants of the Mannor of Dringhouses in the County of York" and dated 1639, contains details of the paines, or fines, which would be imposed on the villagers for various misdemeanours. Requirements concerned, amongst other things: scouring the sewers (ie watercourses), gripping the land (ie putting in small ditches), not cutting hedges or carrying away wood, not ploughing certain areas, sowing and harrowing at specific times, not laying hay within a yard of a chimney, not driving horses or cattle through the west field or horses loose through the northfield, no mares or foals to be tethered in the town field until the corn and hay be "begotten in", not cutting another's grass, and maintaining the common pinfold (where stray animals were secured).

All these and many other matters which are mentioned in the document give a detailed picture of life in this rural community; the Acomb Manor Court Rolls reveal similar preoccupations at this period in Acomb.

The pinfold in Dringhouses. This pinfold is beside Tadcaster Road, opposite Royal Chase. The plaque reads: "This Pinfold, or Pound, was originally an enclosure in which straying cattle were confined pending the payment of a fine. These structures were principally in use in the 17th, 18th and 19th centuries and were generally situated on roadsides and areas of common grazing."

8. 1644: The Siege of York – Scottish Soldiers on Hob Moor

CIVIL WAR BROKE OUT in 1642. By 1644, Scottish and Parliamentarian troops were threatening Charles I's armies in Northern England, and York, a major royalist stronghold, found herself in early June surrounded on all sides by hostile forces. The Scots had marched south from Durham. In Tadcaster they combined with English Parliamentarian troops under the command of the Fairfaxes before approaching York.

The area to the south-west of the city, from near Clifton round to Middlethorpe, was occupied by more than ten thousand Scottish troops under the command of the Earl of Leven. They stayed for ten weeks, many encamped on Hob Moor and presumably using Hob Lane as their principal route to and from the moor. The Earl had his headquarters at Middlethorpe; nearby was the Scots' ordnance depot from which artillery, shot and powder were issued, including for the guns at Acomb.

The Civil War obelisk at Marston Moor.

The Scots became much feared for their ruthlessness, and the residents of Dringhouses, Holgate and Acomb must have had a desperate time. "The Scots are the predominant evil", wrote Charles' Secretary of State. They had vowed not to plunder, but one of the Scottish chaplains wrote of the soldiers taking "much provision from the wind milnes [mills] by the town". There were windmills in the Acomb and Holgate area as well as elsewhere in York, and the present Holgate Windmill, which dates from 1792, is a striking reminder of these important structures. The Scots most probably raided Folly Mill as well.

The Royalist defenders of York held three "sconces" (gun emplacements) outside the city walls to the south-west. Two of these fell to Scottish attacks: "A serjeant and six our souldiers killed before Akham [Acomb]", wrote one of the Scottish commanders. Food was short and illness spread among the ranks. When the Royalist Prince Rupert arrived and broke the siege, the Scots dispersed quickly, a likely sign that they were desperate for fresh provisions.

That could have spelt the end of York's immediate troubles. Instead, Rupert's decision to fight at Marston Moor led to the comprehensive defeat of the Royalists. Soon afterwards, York was forced to surrender to the Parliamentarians.

Holgate Windmill in 1911. The five sails were taken down in 1930 after they were badly damaged in heavy gales. (York City Archives, Acc. 157 Add., 40.2)

9. *What's in a Name?*

ONE OF THE MOST INTRIGUING FEATURES of Hob Moor is its name, together with the presence beside the path on Little Hob Moor of the Hob Stone. The stone is a heavy coffin lid, now set upright, bearing the effigy of a knight. It was sculpted between 1300 and 1317.

We know that the Hob Stone was erected in 1717. Drake, in his *Eboracum* published in 1736, says that the stone had lately been put in place and he quotes the verse inscribed on the back: "This image long Hob's name has bore who was a knight in time of yore and gave this common to ye poor." In the second volume of Nichols' *History and Antiquities of the County of Leicester*, published between 1795 and 1815, there are two engravings, showing the back and the front of the stone; a first date for the erecting of the stone is inscribed: 1717.

Reference to the records in York City Archives of the Wardmote Court, where Constables and Pasture Masters were appointed, reveals that in 1717 the names of the Micklegate Ward Pasture Masters, partly obscured in the engraving by a metal bar, were William Tesh, Lewis Darcy, John Yates and John Lunn.

The second date of 1757 was perhaps added when the stone had to be set upright again. The metal bars have disappeared, leaving just the holes where they were affixed, and the two large stones, which in this engraving form a pedestal for the Hob Stone, had also vanished by 1969, either removed or hidden under tarmacadam.

It is fortunate that we have a further picture of the stone, namely a drawing made in 1825 by George Nicholson (1787–1878). Baptised and buried at Malton, he was a gifted topographical artist who travelled widely in England, France and Italy, working in oils, water colour and pencil as well as producing lithographs and etchings. His pencil sketch of the Hob Stone would appear to give a more accurate representation of the form of the writing of the inscription than does the Nichols' engraving. Nowadays, the lettering is almost totally eroded but the capital letter C of "Common" can still be discerned.

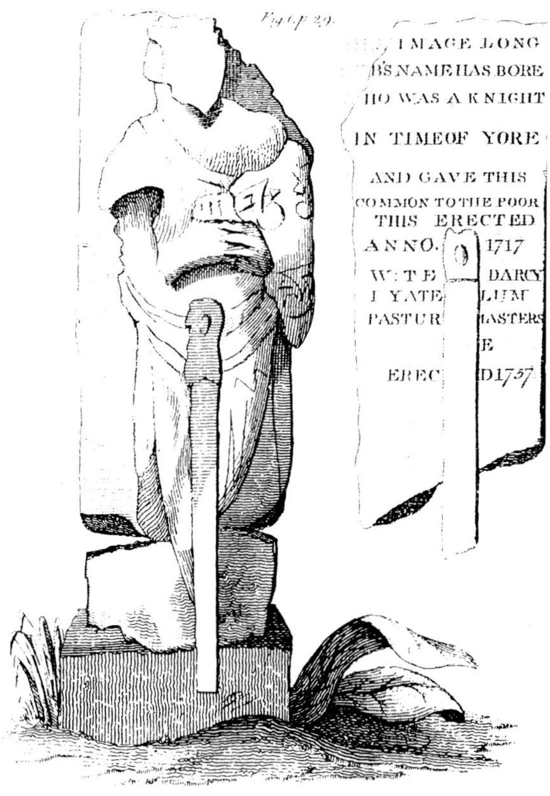

The two engravings of the Hob Stone, from Nichols' "History and Antiquities of the County of Leicester", volume 2, part 1, page 28. (City of York Libraries)

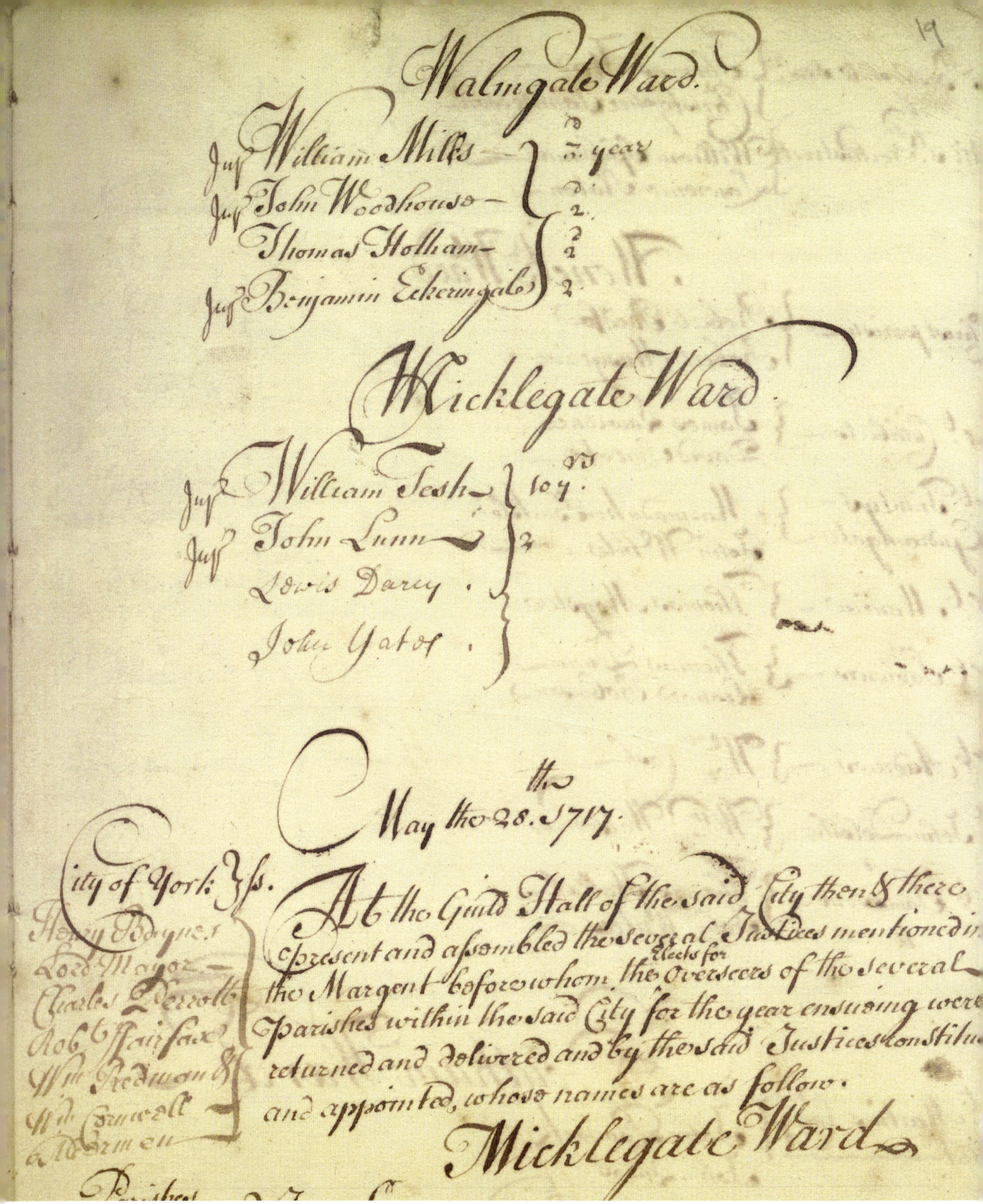

The names of the Micklegate Ward Pasture Masters, 1717. (York City Archives, E101/19)

The front of the Hob Stone today. The head and shoulders can be seen, and the shield covering the knight's left arm.

George Nicholson's sketch of the Hob Stone, 1825. (York Museums Trust (York Art Gallery))

The back of the Hob Stone today. The capital letter C is visible halfway down near the left-hand edge.

It seems clear that the stone was indeed set up, as stated in the inscription, by the Pasture Masters in 1717, but why this was done, and at this precise spot, is far from clear. It is located at the place where Samuel Parsons marked a house on his map in 1624, so maybe it was placed by the last house before one went down the slope to Hob Moor. It is still clearly visible from the main Tadcaster Road so perhaps it was set up to indicate to those passing along that road and seeking Hob Moor that this was the access they were looking for. The back of the stone, with its inscription, faces towards the main road today and presumably always has done. It was obviously important to the Pasture Masters who placed this stone to make an unambiguous statement about the status of Hob Moor to all who approached.

The Pasture Masters were correct in stating that Hob Moor was a common but the rest of the inscription is not necessarily true. The effigy is that of a knight of the Ros family who had extensive connections in Yorkshire. Their arms, with three water-bougets (a yoke supporting two leather water-bags), appear on the Hob Stone effigy and in 14th-century stained glass in Holy Trinity Church, Goodramgate (now in the care of the Churches Conservation Trust). They can also be seen in several places in York Minster, including on the second and third arches of the north aisle; individual water bougets can also be seen in the donor panels of the magnificent St William Window.

The shield also appears on the arch at Kirkham Priory; on a large framed canvas, dated 1576, of the Ten Commandments in the church at Kirk Deighton, near Wetherby; and in London at the Temple Church, the headquarters of the Order of the Knights Templar, of which members of the Ros family were patrons. The Order was founded in 1119 to protect pilgrims in the Holy Land and was established throughout Europe by the late 13th century. Opinion turned against them however after their failure in 1291 to prevent the fall of the last Christian stronghold in the Holy Land and in 1309–10, the Templars of northern England were imprisoned in York Castle. The Order was finally dissolved everywhere in 1312.

The Ros family had strong connections nationwide with, for example, places in Northumberland, Cumberland and Leicestershire, and with Scarborough and Helmsley in Yorkshire. They owned property in Coney Street, York, and at Ingmanthorpe, Ribston and Kirk Deighton, where there is a grave slab with Latin inscriptions concerning Robert Ros, who died 22 April 1476, and his wife Maria. There were at least two barons called Robert de Ros; one was amongst the twenty-five witnesses of the signing of the Magna Carta at Runnymede in 1215. Indeed, the name of Ros or Roos appears in nearly all the great events of the 12th, 13th and 14th centuries.

Now, "Hob" is the familiar form, from Middle English, of "Rob", short for Robert or Robin; the Hob Stone inscription tells us that Hob, a knight, gave the common to the poor. However, although the Ros family made gifts of land, no evidence has as yet been found of a historical link between Hob Moor and any Robert de Ros. On the contrary, William I'Anson considered that the Hob Stone effigy is of the first William de Ros of Ingmanthorpe, who died in 1310 and was buried in the church of the Grey Friars, York. A full explanation of the history of this effigy and of its true connection with Hob Moor remains, for the time being, elusive.

For centuries, the name Yorks (or Yorke) Moor was used in official documents and was only gradually superseded by Hob Moor. Perhaps the villagers had always known the area as Hob Moor, whereas the City authorities had wished to stress that the area belonged to York. Be this as it may, "Hob" is a common element in place-names, especially in North Yorkshire and Derbyshire. Notwithstanding the inscription made by the Pasture Masters in 1717, it is possible to seek an alternative explanation of the name of Hob Moor.

A belief in fairies was widely held during the Middle Ages and beyond, and one of the standard fairies of English folklore is the brownie, or hob, a sprite that helps housewives. However, the hob is notoriously hard to please, easily offended and capricious; some are malevolent by nature, others turn so. On the whole, it was believed that a hob is hostile to mankind; "Hob" also means Devil. Likewise in English folklore, Robin Goodfellow, half fairy and half human, is also a mischievous sprite and, as we have seen, "Hob" is the familiar form of "Rob", short for Robin as well as for Robert. Robin Goodfellow is a trickster, but not a household one; he is a will-o'-the-wisp, a marsh-spirit or moor-spirit. Small flames flickering over marshy ground, caused by self-igniting gases from decaying plants, gave rise to this widespread belief.

The Ancient Common was a large area of featureless, poorly drained grassland with boundaries that must have looked very alike. Today we have some housing, the railway line, the swimming baths and the fences round the school sites to help us to know whereabouts on the Moor we are, but in days of yore things must have been very different. If the sun, moon, stars or Minster were not in sight, it must have been only too easy, even in reasonable weather conditions, to lose one's sense of direction, the more so in rain or mist. Perhaps this is how the Moor gained its name: a remote place where Robin Goodfellow, or Hob, played tricks, making people lose their way.

What's in a name? In the case of Hob Moor, a long, fascinating history and a tantalising glimpse of our distant past.

Robin Goodfellow, adapted from the 17th century "black-letter ballad" (Payne Knight, 1865, plate 37(2)). (By permission of The British Library; Cup.820.I.18) (Swea Sayers)

10. *The Tadcaster-York Turnpike*

DURING THE 18TH CENTURY, it became obvious that the system whereby parishes and townships were responsible for the maintenance of highways was no longer able to cope. Turnpike Trusts were therefore set up to maintain and improve individual stretches of highway and had the power to levy tolls. The term "turnpike" originated in an older practice of turning the pike, which formed the barrier to traffic, to allow access. Each Turnpike Trust was established by a separate Act of Parliament; in 1820, over 1000 trusts were controlling some 22,000 miles of roads in Britain, the network being entirely the result of local initiatives.

The shortest and busiest route in the toll network centred on York was the Tadcaster to York road, which still forms one of the boundaries of Little Hob Moor. It was the first to be established, in 1745, and was discontinued in 1872. Its end-points were Tadcaster Bridge and "Hob Moor Lane End", the latter being the place at which the turnpike met the city boundary; a boundary stone is still in situ beside Tadcaster Road opposite the end of the lane.

Turnpike milestones, erected 1820.

It seems that shortly after the trust began work on this turnpike, the City authorities felt obliged to improve the standard of the road on their side of the boundary. In the Minutes of a Council Meeting held on 9 December 1747, the following was recorded:

> Ordered that Eighty four pounds eleven shillings and seven pence shall be paid to Mr Henry Driffield out of the Comon Chamber of this City ... for day's wages and labour (to) be paid to Workmen for labour and loading and ... for his own trouble care and attendance in making a Way like the Turnpike Road from the end of the City's broad Cawsway to Hob lane end where the Turnpike Road begins in pursuance of the Order of this House of the 9th of May 1746.

The 1852 map shows that a weighing machine and the turnpike were located in Dringhouses on the further side from York, thus enabling York citizens to travel toll-free as far as there. Combined milestones and mounting blocks were erected in 1772 and then replaced in 1820 with milestones bearing cast-iron inscriptions giving the distance measured from Ouse Bridge. Each milestone also bears the name of the road: **"Tadcaster and Hob Moor Road"**, together with the name of a nearby locality, for example York City, Dringhouses, Askham Bryan.

Toll revenues declined with the coming of the railways, leading inexorably to the demise of the Turnpike Trusts, but several local milestones are still in place, proclaiming the existence of Hob Moor and reminding the passer-by of the era of stagecoaches.

A stagecoach dating from the 1820s. This stagecoach, which can be seen in Kirkgate, York Castle Museum, is typical of those in use at the time. Four people travelled inside and ten outside. (York Museums Trust (York Castle Museum))

11. The Ancient Common under the Plough

THE LONG LINES OF RIDGE AND FURROW which cover the whole of the Ancient Common area are by far the most extensive historical landscape feature on Hob Moor. They are strikingly different from the medieval ridge and furrow that can be seen, for instance, in North Lane Pasture, and that were made by a plough drawn by oxen. The furrows on the Ancient Common were cut by horse-ploughing; the lines are straight and parallel and the ridges close together. They are known as "narrow rig", sometimes as "Napoleonic ridge and furrow". The latter name arose because they were created at the very beginning of the 19th century, when England was struggling to overcome Napoleon's domination of Europe.

Horse-ploughing in the early 1800s. (W H Pyne, 1802; reproduced by kind permission of The Rural History Centre, University of Reading)

"Narrow rig" on the western part of the Ancient Common, clearly visible after heavy rain.

Archaeological aerial photograph of the western part of Hob Moor. (Anthony Crawshaw)

By the end of the 18th century, York had become a centre of fashion in the North and a resort for the genteel, yet in parts of the city there were areas of considerable poverty. The population was rising sharply and jobs were scarce. There were few new industries in York. The wars against France (1793–1815) created new problems: rents rose rapidly, taxation was increased and the price of corn was particularly high as a result of disastrous harvests in 1809 and 1811. Corporation records state that the poor in York at this time, "not being properly supplied with work, are become highly burthensome".

The creation of "narrow rig" on Hob Moor (and on other areas of the York Strays) was most probably a response to these economic crises. The City authorities would have been alarmed by reports of popular disturbances involving machine-breaking (Luddism) in a number of West Yorkshire towns, as well as the spiralling costs of poor relief. The creation of a community supply of grain to be used as a supplement to the administration of poor relief would have seemed an attractive idea, and it seems likely that the Pasture Masters, on behalf of the ward freemen, would have collected rent from the Corporation in exchange for this temporary loss of pasture facilities.

The archaeological aerial photograph of the western part of Hob Moor was taken during the afternoon in winter (5 December 1999) as landscape features show up particularly well when the sun is low in the sky and when the grass is short. The medieval ridge and furrow in North Lane Pasture shows up less well because of its orientation, but the "narrow rig", which is aligned east-west, can be seen distinctly on the Ancient Common, extending right up to the line of the former city boundary in the south-west corner. (See the 1852 Ordnance Survey map on page 45.) To the north of Our Lady's School can be seen more medieval ridge and furrow in former open fields, now partly included in Hob Moor and partly in the grounds of Hob Moor School.

This one-horse plough was in use at Appleton Roebuck during the 1930s and 1940s; it is now in a garden in Acomb. Its larger furrow wheel was lost and has been replaced by a second land wheel. The design of the plough evolved only very slowly from the Middle Ages (see the illustration from the Luttrell Psalter on page 25) until the advent of the mechanised plough in the 1950s.

12. *The Old Causeway*

THE AERIAL PHOTOGRAPH on page 42 shows very clearly part of the main track across Hob Moor. Its full length is from near the corner of the old city boundary to the north-east corner, where today a snicket links it to Holly Bank Road.

The 1852 6" Ordnance Survey map shows the line of this causeway, with a footbridge at each end, as being part of a footpath which follows a remarkably straight line from Askham Bryan to The Mount area.

Close examination of the aerial photograph shows that, although the causeway cuts across the "narrow rig" for most of its length and seems to have been re-profiled in fairly recent times, at its south-west end the ridges and furrows are intact. This means that the causeway on Hob Moor predates the Napoleonic Wars. At the south-west end, the footpath is obliged to make a small diversion from the straight line, but the manner in which it then crosses the fields, whose boundaries were established following the 1774–6 Acomb and Holgate Enclosure Acts, shows that it predates that enclosure.

Between roughly 1750 and 1850, enclosure of open fields, commons and wastes transformed the landscape. The scattered strips belonging to an individual owner were replaced by a field (or fields), bounded by fences or hedges drawn in straight lines, in which communal farming practices were superseded by the individual farmer controlling his own crops

The main track, looking north-east towards the Minster.

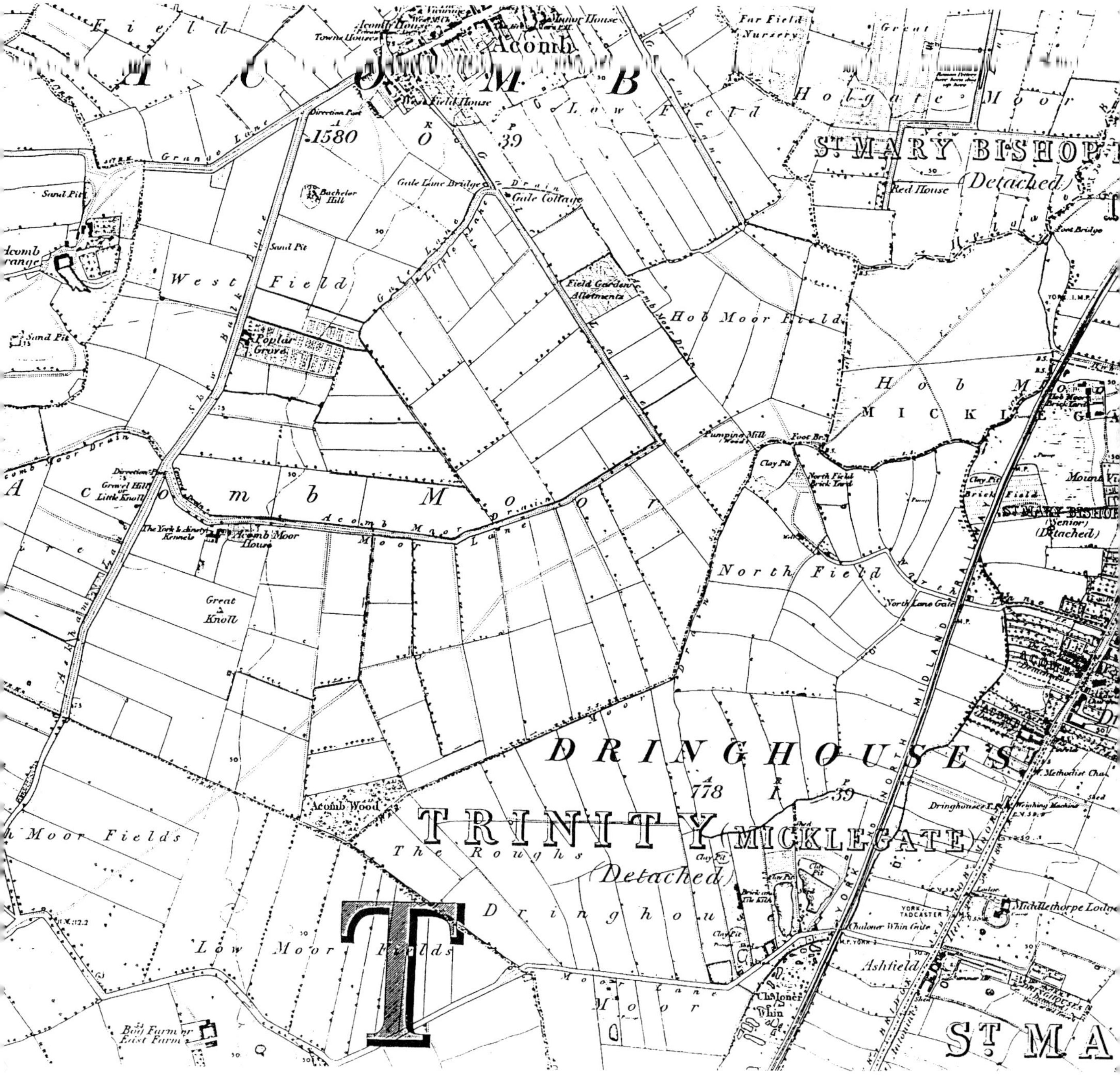

Part of sheet 174 of the 1852 6" Ordnance Survey:1 mile map, reduced, showing the footpath crossing Hob Moor and going across the fields towards Askham Bryan. (York City Archives)

and stock. The distinctive pattern of post-Enclosure fields, more or less square or rectangular, is shown well on this 1852 map.

Earlier direct evidence of the existence of the causeway on Hob Moor is very difficult to find. In two descriptions of the boundaries of the City of York (1374 and 1500), an "outgang" (trackway) is mentioned in connection with Hob Moor, but in neither instance is it possible to say with any certainty that the access referred to was connected with the causeway.

However, in 1602 the City undertook to repair "a stone bridge and a wooden bridge and the cawsey adjoining the said wooden bridge in the lane leading to Hob Moor called Hob Lane", leading to the (said) mill. From this it would appear that the wooden bridge spanned the beck at the bottom of Hob Lane and that the stone bridge was nearby. It seems not unreasonable to assume that this second bridge was in the north-east corner of Hob Moor. Such a bridge would probably have been similar to a packhorse bridge: narrow, allowing only one animal at a time to pass across it; it would have had one arch and probably no parapet. Perhaps it was similar to the old bridge at Sinnington.

There is a documentary reference dated 1664 to "Folly Milne Brigg, situate upon Hob Moor" in a description of the boundary of Holgate town, township and territories, and the bridge was at the point where the Holgate Beck turns to flow northwards into the Ouse, presumably very near the mill of the same name. It is possible to surmise that the causeway came into being, if not in much earlier times, then sometime in the Middle Ages, maybe as part of a direct packhorse route or footpath from York's hinterland into the city, and that the stone bridge, the mill and the causeway were closely associated. A mill was an important building and required good access.

The old bridge at Sinnington, near Kirkbymoorside. (P Walker)

13. *Little Hob Moor: Brickmaking, Cottages and Allotments*

Brickmaking

THERE ARE THREE early references to the existence of clayworking in Dringhouses. In the Poll Tax list for 1379, there is Willelmus Watson, Tyghler (tiler/brickmaker), and in the list of freemen of York for 1430–1 there is Henricus Drynghouse, potter; "clay pytts" are mentioned in the document from 1563 concerning the lease of "Hobmylne and a closse". For the time being, however, the location of the earliest clay pits remains a matter of conjecture.

The earliest precise evidence of brickworking in Dringhouses is to be found on the plan accompanying the Dringhouses Inclosures Award in 1822; the south-west part of Little Hob Moor is given the name "Brick Garth". Subsequently, a plan drawn in 1838 of the Middlethorpe and Dringhouses Estates belonging to the Reverend Edward Trafford Leigh shows Hob Moor Brick Yard as including not only part of Little Hob Moor but also extending on the west side of the railway line, built in 1836. It would appear that the brickyard had already been extended over the whole of this area up to the boundary of the Ancient Common before the coming of the railway.

The 1852 6" Ordnance Survey map (see page 45) shows Hob Moor Brick Yard, and a clay pit as part of a Brick Field straddling the railway line.

The 1:2500 Ordnance Survey "First Edition" map of 1892 shows the full extent of the Hob Moor brick works.The clay workings had by this time been extended southwards as far as North Lane (now re-named Mayfield Grove here) and some of them worked out; the earlier workings on the west side of the railway had now become "Old Clay Pits", and the area of Little Hob Moor called "Brick Garth" on the 1822 plan had terraced housing on it and was still part of the "Hobmoor Brick Works" site.

In Kelly's *Directory* of 1861, it was stated that in Dringhouses, "bricks and tiles of good quality are made in the neighbourhood". Between 1877 and 1889, there were at least three brick manufacturers in Dringhouses, including the firm of Nelson (hence Nelson's Lane). The brick works were taken over by builders, including the Biscomb brothers who in 1904 won the contract to build Poppleton Road School. In general, brick manufacture thrived particularly well in the Victorian era; after the Second World War, the smaller firms went out of business when they found they were unable to compete with the lower prices of the larger firms who could exploit economy of scale.

Cottages

In August 1889, Rutter and Co submitted plans for a new street near Hob Moor; twenty-nine dwellings were originally proposed but only eighteen were built, forming Hob Moor Terrace, Vernon Street and Rutter Street, as marked on the Ordnance Survey "First Edition" map of 1892.

In the early 1970s, the thirteen houses which had been built at the northern end of the brick-works area (on the early "Brick Garth"), were demolished; a group of five houses was left and they are still there, at the northern end of the present Hob Moor Terrace.

STRAY
F.P.
S.D.
6ft. R.H.
1a
·022
RUTTER STREET
Tank
VERNON STREET
HOBMOOR TERRACE
1
4·214
Hobmoor Brick Works
72
1·904
Und
Hob's S
B.M.62·1
2
5·979
3
1·141
6
1·399
5
8·878
B.M.50·2
10
2·372
Old
Clay Pit
11
5·662
Old
Clay Pits
9
8·120
8
·840
387
B.M.51·0
B.M.67
Brick Yard
Brick Yard
12
5·556
Brick Kiln
Brick &
Tile Works
Incline
13
6·077
Def.
17
·975
16
1·081
15
1·737
Clay Pit
Def.
F.P.
4 ft. R.H.
6
·307
3
4·166
Clay Pit
5
·402
2
·819
B.S.
Def.
L A N E
4
·396
North Eastern
Terrace
Turf
Tavern
The H
Roman Tomb

Opposite: 1:2500 Ordnance Survey "First Edition" map, 1892 (slightly reduced), showing the Hob Moor Brick Works. (York City Archives)

The cottages of Rutter Street and no. 1, Hob Moor Terrace in the 1970s. Railway signals and rolling stock can be seen in the background. (York City Archives, Acc.157 Add., Album 27)

Although the other dwellings were demolished, traces of their existence can be seen at times. After a prolonged period of dry weather, the lines of their foundations are visible where the soil is shallow and the grass becomes parched.

Parched lines in grass showing location of former housing, Little Hob Moor.

Hob Moor Terrace. Old houses as they look today.

Allotments

Adjacent to Tadcaster Road on Little Hob Moor, there is an area of allotments. Such small plots of land, originally provided for the growing of vegetables, were first created in the late 18th century; by 1833, 42% of parishes had some allotments; in 1887, as a result of the general concern regarding mass migration from country to town and the lack of gardens for the back-to-back housing, the Allotments Act enabled local authorities to purchase land for allotments. As a result of such provision being made also by landowners, by 1900 there were nearly half a million allotments in England and Wales, and the number increased further during the Great War, when food production was crucial.

In York, the Minutes of the Parks and Small Holdings Committee, 1916–17, mention War-time Allotments and the provision of further allotments; in April 1918, the Committee gave the City Engineer "certain instructions with regard to the fencing round the Hob Moor allotments and the approach road to the allotments", from which it seems reasonable to conclude that the plots were created at about that time. They were just a few of the one and a half million which by then existed. After the 1950s, there was an accelerating decline in the number of allotments nationally and there are now just over a quarter of a million. Those created on Little Hob Moor during the Great War are still there, continuing to provide vegetables, fruit and flowers, an evening and weekend retreat, companionship with fellow allotment-holders and relaxation.

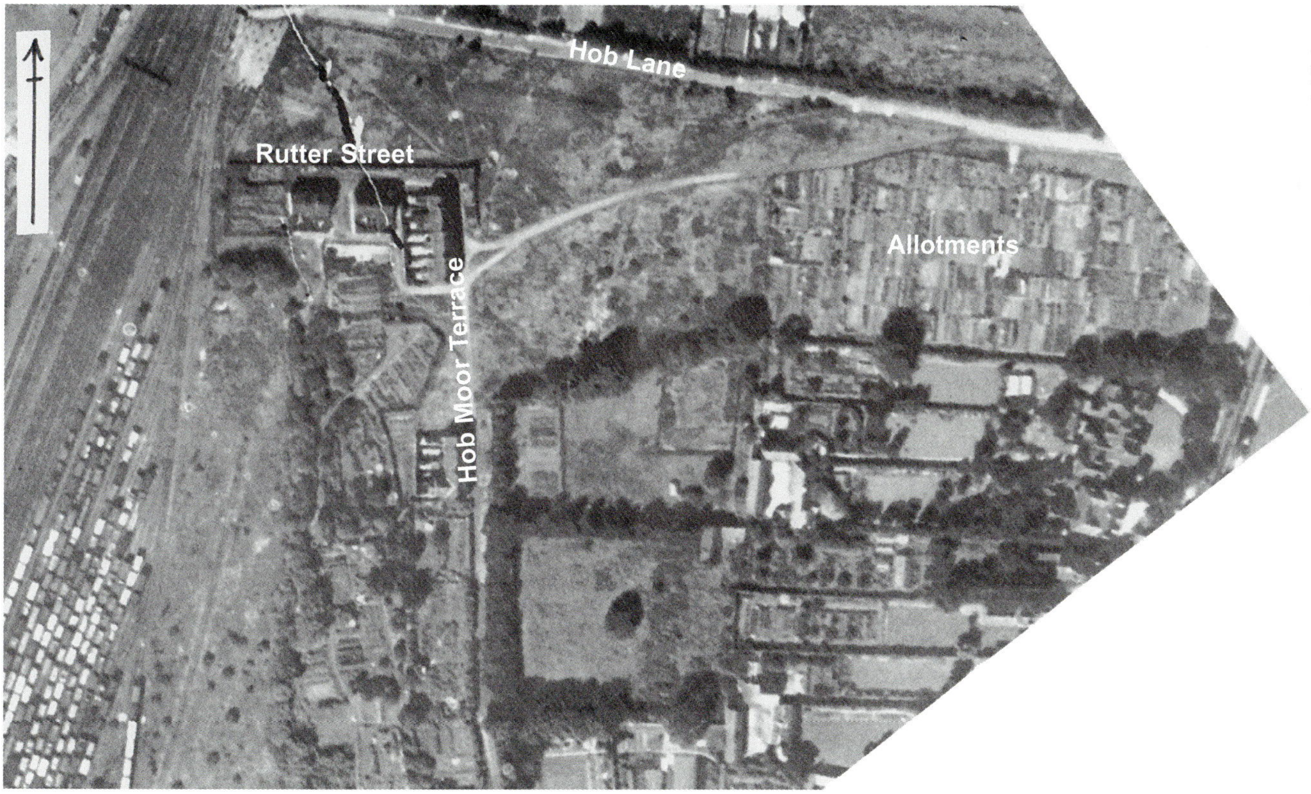

This 1936 aerial photograph of Little Hob Moor and the former Hob Moor Brick Works area shows the Vernon Street, Rutter Street and Hob Moor Terrace housing and the allotments. The remainder of Little Hob Moor is rough ground, not the regularly mown grassland which we see today. (York City Archives)

14. Kelsey's Pond

THE SOUTH-WEST PART of Hob Moor (behind the Edmund Wilson Baths) has seen big changes over the last two hundred years. On the 1852 6" Ordnance Survey map, it is already a well-established brickyard, being named as the North Field Brick Yard, with Clay Pit and Pumping Mill (see the map on page 45). By 1892 the clay pit had doubled in size and there were two pumping mills and a kiln. By 1909 the clay pit had reached its maximum size of 6.6 acres and may already have filled with water, as the windpumps are shown on the map as being "old", there is no kiln marked, and other clay pits have appeared nearby.

The Ordnance Survey map revised in 1937 shows how much the area of open water had diminished; some disused clay pits had been used in part as rubbish pits and were gradually becoming marshland, whilst clay was now being dug out of new pits to the west of Acomb Moor brick works. However, the original clay pit, with its two windpumps, remained as Kelsey's Pond, of which many people have fond memories.

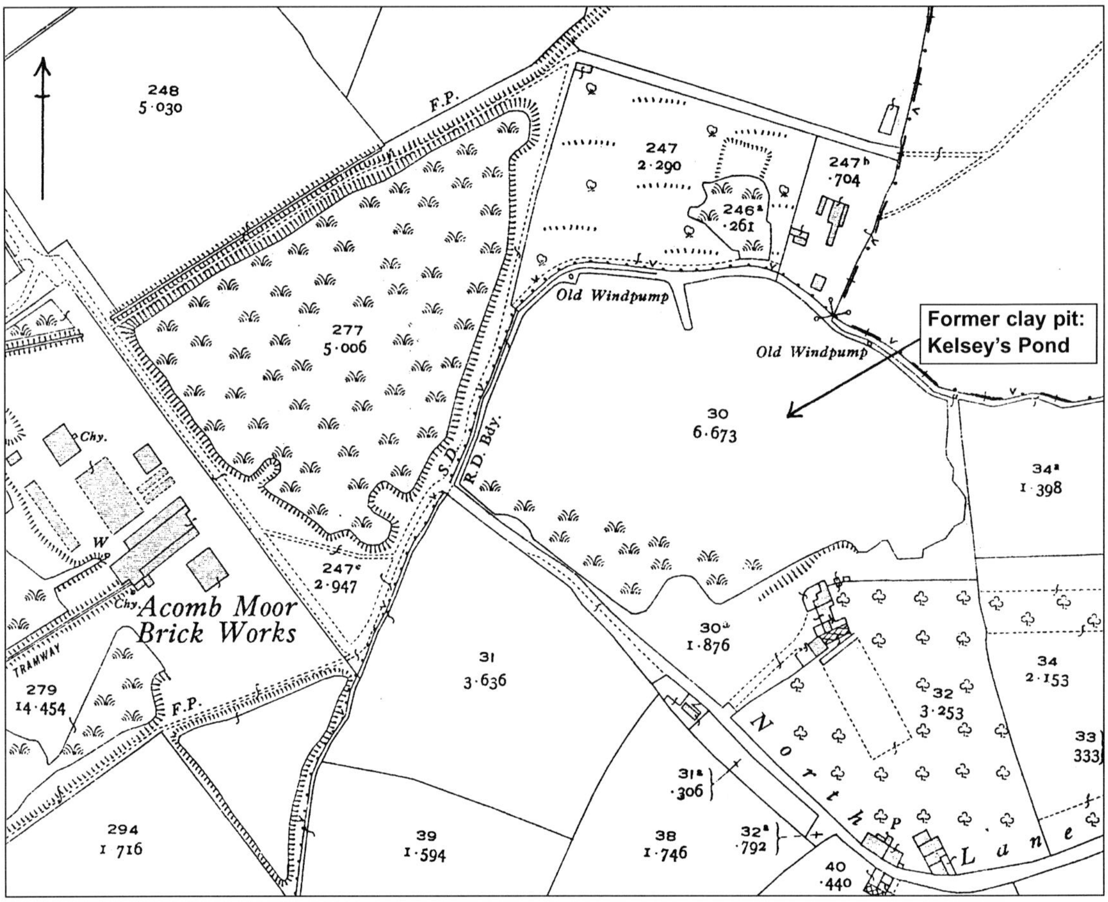

Part of the 1931 1:2500 Ordnance Survey map, revised 1929 (reduced). (York City Archives)

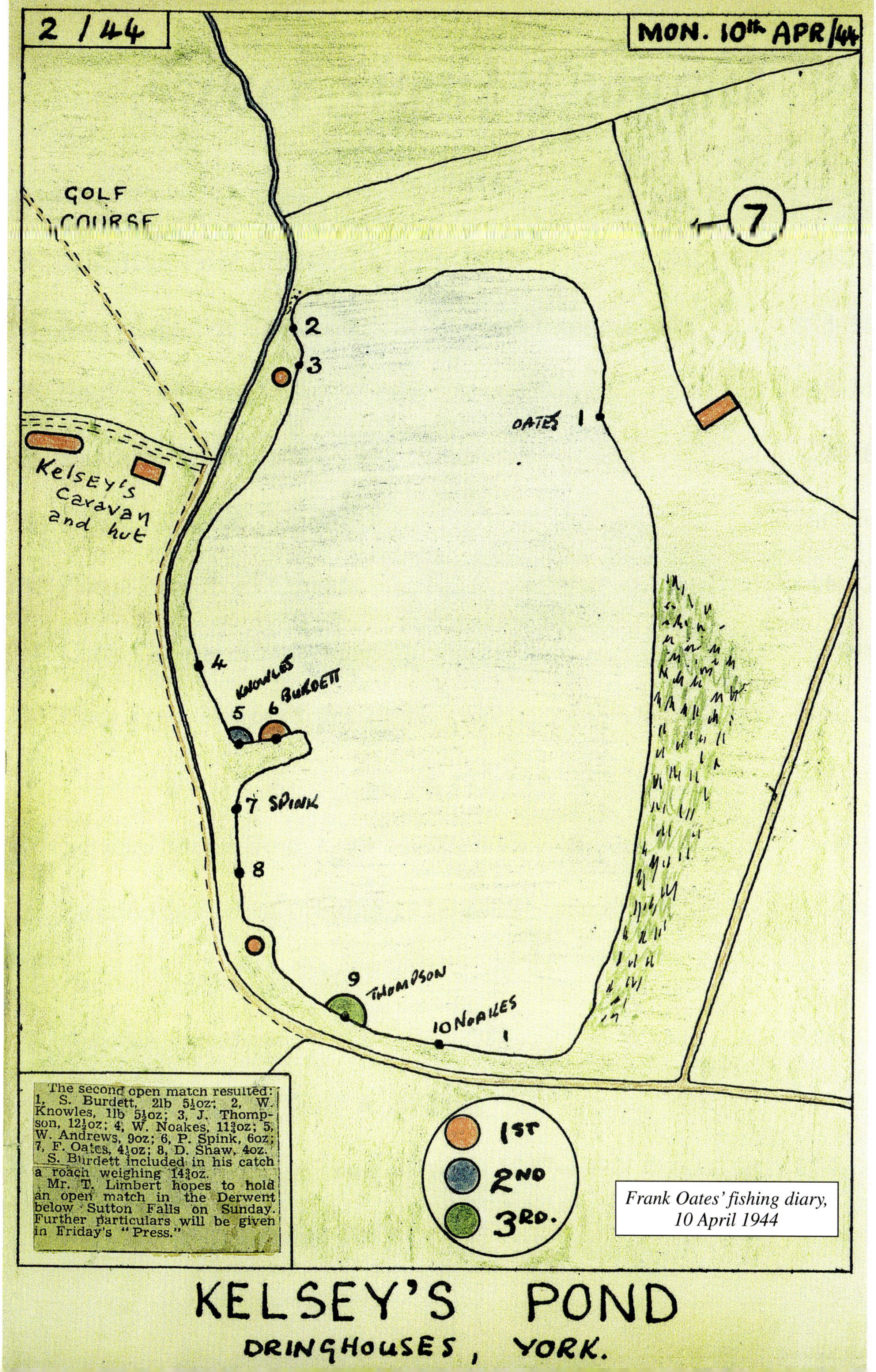

Frank Oates' fishing diary, 10 April 1944

Mute swans nesting on Kelsey's Pond, photographed by Frank Oates in 1947. One of the old windpumps can be seen on the far side of the pond.

Mr Harry Kelsey lived with his family in a bungalow with a verandah, only a few yards to the north of the pond. He used to go round the pond with a large hook, pulling the weed out. Although the pond was man-made, it looked entirely natural, surrounded by trees and bulrushes. The local lads used to go fishing, paying 6d a day; some enthusiasts would be there from four o'clock in the morning, when it was still misty; the fish included tench, roach, perch, bream, carp and pike. Fishing matches were very popular and anglers would come from as far afield as Leeds to compete. Frank Oates was one of those who regularly took part in these events, and he kept a detailed fishing diary, of which the page for Monday 10 April 1944 is reproduced here; it shows where each fisherman sat, the windpumps, Mr Kelsey's caravan and hut, and the golf course (on Hob Moor).

People used to skate on Kelsey's Pond; one year, the ice was thick enough for about a hundred people to be on it at once. Someone would bring a wind-up gramophone and there would be skating to music.

This beautiful wildlife habitat was destroyed in the 1950s.

In 1824 three fields between Hob Moor and North Lane, on the south side of the Ancient Common, were bought by the Mayor and Commonalty (in their capacity as Trustees acting on behalf of the Freemen) and became part of Hob Moor. In early 1941 the field nearest to the railway was requisitioned for the construction of a cold store. After the war, the Ministry of Foods and later the Ministry of Works sought to acquire this site in exchange for another piece of land. After protracted negotiations, in June 1954 a proposal was to be put by the Parks Committee to the Ministry of Works that "the Gale Lane tip land complete and incomplete should be appropriated for Parks purposes and the purposes of the City of York (Micklegate Strays) Act, 1907 at the cost of the Ministry together with a payment in respect of the levelling and soiling and re-seeding of this tip. The land adjoins the Hob Moor and would make an excellent extension thereto." Kelsey's Pond had been backfilled over a period of years and for many local people this process was heartbreaking.

Thus, in exchange for the land of the cold store site, Hob Moor was extended south-westwards to Thanet Road; later, the Edmund Wilson Baths were built on a small part of the tip land.

15. *The Golf Course*

THE FIRST MENTION of members of the North Eastern Railway Institute being able to play golf on Hob Moor is in the Corporation's Parks Committee Minutes of November 1918. The application for the laying out of the course was received in February 1920 and during that year the course was constructed. There were nine holes, over the area of the Ancient Common, and the Institute paid rent of £1 per hole per annum.

Already at the end of that first year the Committee was recommending that the Club should not be allowed to cut the fairways, as "this would destroy a very large amount of eatage on the Moor and the rent proposed to be paid would not be adequate". The depasturing of cattle and horses on the moor (usually during the Races, when they were transferred from the Knavesmire), and which areas could be cut, were only two of the ongoing conflicts of interest which arose. Other matters included complaints that children were "damaging the greens by playing cricket etc. thereon"; bunkers being made on the Moor in breach of the tenancy agreement; the number of times and exactly when the grass could be cut on the fairways and generally; whether the Club should be charged rates; the use of a hut by Club personnel as a dwelling house; the number of holes; and more cattle being transferred from the Knavesmire during the period of a Military Tattoo being held there in 1926. No money was given during such periods by the Committee to help with the extra fencing needed round the greens.

One animal was welcomed – indeed, even introduced by the Club – onto Hob Moor: a horse called Scamp. Scamp was bought for £18 in 1922 to work on the course; from time to time, he was also loaned out, on a "meat for work" basis. However, his accommodation apparently presented problems. He was temporarily "stalled" in 1925 at Bungalow Farm; later the same year, a carriage roof was erected as a bicycle shed for members' use but it was decided as a temporary measure to use the cycle shed as a stable for the horse. Scamp had to be destroyed in 1926; his replacement was stabled at the Cross Keys public house in Dringhouses, but this horse was sold for £17.10.0d in December of the same year and replaced by a Dennis motor mower. The following year, the course was rolled by hiring a horse for two days and, following the removal of the cattle, a horse was again needed when the rough areas needed to be cut.

The Parks Committee regulated the fee charged by the Club to non-members. In January 1924, it was requested by the Club that the rights of the general public to play on Hob Moor should be subject to the members having preference on Bank Holidays, Saturdays and days on which competitions were to be held, and the Committee agreed to this.

In 1932 and 1933, the Parks Committee had bought extra fields adjacent to Hob Moor at the western side and in June 1934 these were taken into the golf course.

The plan of the golf course dated 11 May 1935 shows the layout of the course in detail; the extended area also included The Triangle, with two bridges over the beck, one wide enough to take the mowing machine across. Greens 6, 8 and 15 can still be seen on the ground and 6 and 8 are visible on the aerial photograph on page 42.

Railway Institute Golf Club – York.

Hob Moor Course.

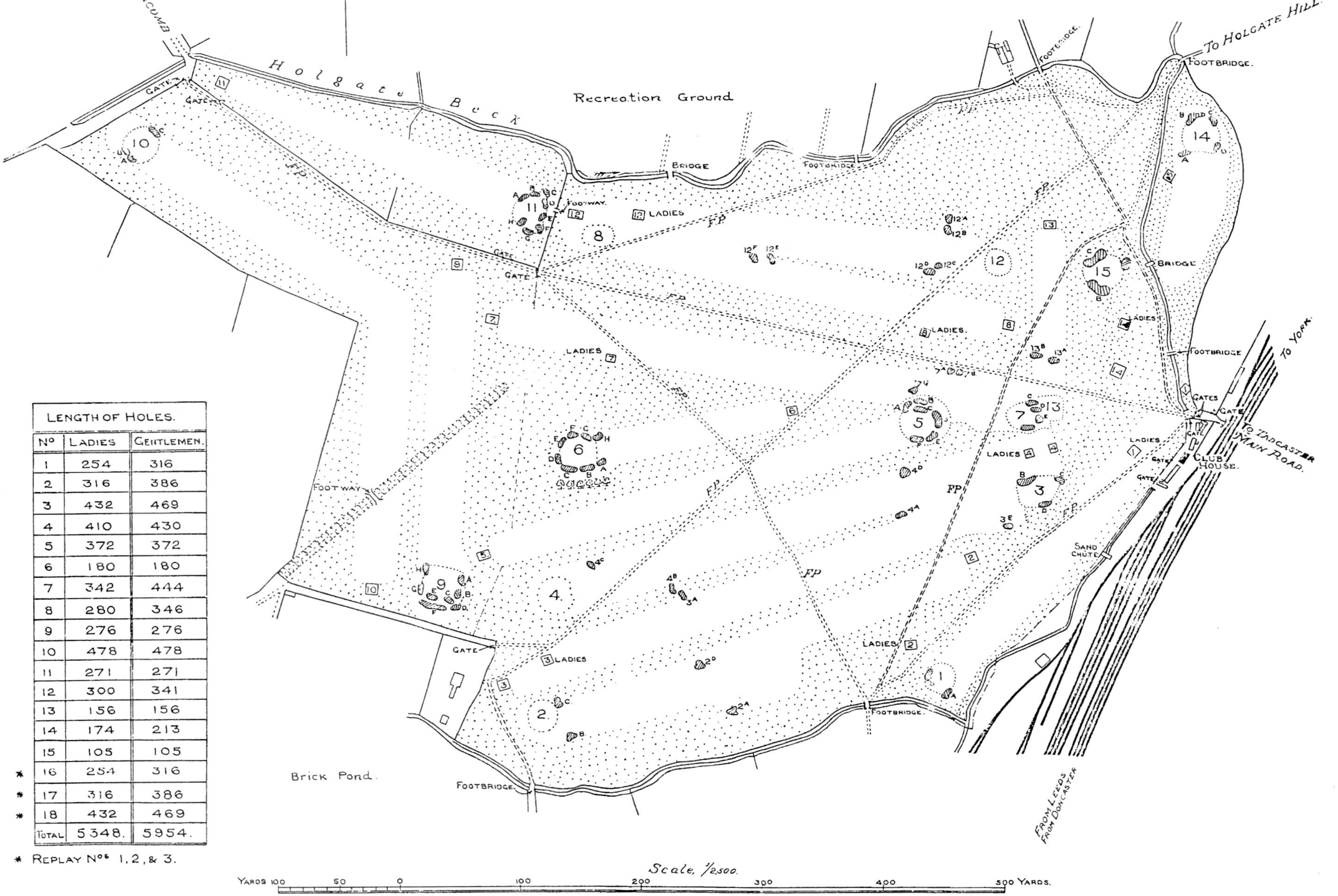

Length of Holes.		
Nº	Ladies	Gentlemen.
1	254	316
2	316	386
3	432	469
4	410	430
5	372	372
6	180	180
7	342	444
8	280	346
9	276	276
10	478	478
11	271	271
12	300	341
13	156	156
14	174	213
15	105	105
* 16	254	316
* 17	316	386
* 18	432	469
Total	5348.	5954.

* Replay Nos 1, 2, & 3.

Opposite: Railway Institute Golf Club, York – Hob Moor Golf Course: the 1935 Plan (reduced). (Pike Hills Golf Club)

Green no. 15 today, between the underpass and the Holly Bank access.

Golf Club members outside the clubhouse in the 1930s. This photograph was probably taken by the club photographer and is reproduced here by kind permission of Hugh Murray.

As shown on the plan, the new clubhouse, opened in 1929, and the house for the professional and the greenkeeper were near to the underpass. The accommodation consisted of a hut and railway carriages which had been lifted down from the railway track nearby.

The Railway Institute Golf Club was very popular; the membership grew from thirty-three in 1920 to 200 in 1921–2; by 1933 there was a waiting list and by 1939 there were approaching 400 members. Problems caused by children grew with the increased housing provision nearby such that a children's play area was created on an adjacent area; notices were put up requesting the public not to use the greens and fairways for games. Cattle being depastured on the Moor continued to provide problems and by 1938 the Club was already seeking land elsewhere in the area in order to vacate Hob Moor. However, after the outbreak of war in September 1939, the whole idea of moving was suspended until conditions were "more favourable".

During the war, the problems of damage by children continued and 21 acres (the area to the west taken into the course in 1934) were given up by the Club for grazing. From May 1942, cattle were on the Moor throughout the summer; the greens were protected by fences but the rest of the course was trampled by the cattle and no cutting of the fairways was allowed, to ensure maximum "eatage" for the animals. The members of the Club accepted the difficulties; they felt fortunate to be playing at all "in the present emergency". The Club's Annual Report for 1945 reveals the circumstances of those times.

Given all the problems, including many burglaries at the clubhouse over the years, members were anxious to find a new venue as soon as possible after the end of hostilities. The Club removed to Pike Hills in September 1946. The greens on Hob Moor were of Cumberland turf, a special grass: slow-growing, short, dense, with a narrow blade, and springy. It had been brought in rolls from Cumberland, and when the Railway Institute Golf Club transferred to Pike Hills, various locals appropriated this turf for their gardens. The bunkers were levelled by the Corporation in preparation for football pitches to be marked out, and a new era began.

YORK RAILWAY INSTITUTE GOLF CLUB.

ANNUAL REPORT FOR 1 9 4 5.

Mr. Chairman, Ladies and Gentlemen,

I have pleasure in presenting the 26th. Annual Report of the York Railway Institute Golf Club.

I was elected to the post of Hon. Secretary shortly after the commencement of the War and throughout the War years I have invariably concluded my report by expressing the hope that the one for the following year would be given under peace-time conditions. This wish has at last been realised and I am sure we are all profoundly grateful for this fact.

The task of keeping the Club going during the War has not been an easy one. By 1942 we had been deprived of all our staff with the exception of an old gentleman of over 70 years of age who was our Club House Attendant. In addition we had to allow the course to be used for grazing cattle for six or eight months each year and extra work was caused by the necessity of erecting fencing round the greens. Added to this were the difficulties of maintaining our machinery; in getting repairs done, obtaining spare parts and fuel and the difficulty of transport. I should therefore like to express my very great appreciation of the work of our Professional, Tom Wilson and our Greenkeeper Dalton. During the past three years of the War they have both been working long hours in War-time jobs and they have sacrificed a great deal of their very limited spare time to enable us to maintain the course in playable condition. I know that Tom Wilson has frequently gone straight from his work and before having a meal, in order to use the remaining hours of daylight, has done 2 or 3 hours work on the course. I understand that he has found a bottle of Guinness to be very sustaining on these occasions. Dalton, too, has frequently put in several hours work on the course after working a 10 or 12 hour night shift on his War job. Without the help of these two members of our pre-war staff, I do not think we should have been able to carry on. Had the Club ceased to function a great many of our members would, no doubt, have joined other clubs, or found other interests and given the game up entirely, and the task of reviving the Institute Club would have been a very formidable one. At the same time I should like to pay a very sincere tribute to the members who have continued to support the Club during these difficult years and have accepted the very inferior conditions without complaint. By their loyalty they have played as great a part in keeping the Club going.

-1-

York Railway Institute Golf Club: the first page of the 1945 Annual Report. (Pike Hills Golf Club)

16. Miscellany

Sport

WHEN THE RAILWAY INSTITUTE GOLF CLUB vacated Hob Moor in 1946, York Rugby Union Football Club rented a pitch on Hob Moor. The latter had been founded in 1928 but had no permanent "home" up to the outbreak of war in 1939. Following the end of hostilities, and with many former players returning from the Services, a meeting took place at the Adelphi Hotel and it was decided to rent a pitch on Hob Moor from the Corporation. The rugby club took over two railway carriages which had been locker rooms for the golf club. Eventually funds were raised to purchase, from the Railway Company, the Institute golf clubhouse, for the sum of £300. The rugby club was officially opened on 20 December 1947. It remained at Hob Moor until, in September 1966, it joined with York Cricket Club to set up a new sports complex at Clifton Park on Shipton Road.

Dringhouses Football Club requested a football field on Hob Moor in 1946, and in June 1948 there was mention of cricket pitches on Hob Moor. Football teams have continued to play on the Moor up to the present day.

In April 1982, a proposal for a Municipal Golf Course on Hob Moor was put forward but it was withdrawn the following month.

An Aerodrome proposed for Hob Moor

The idea of a municipal aerodrome being sited on Hob Moor was first mooted in March 1927 and between 1929 and 1933 was under serious consideration by the Corporation. Hob

Football game in progress, October 2003.

Moor was not a big enough area, but the addition of fields to the south and west could have made it into "a good aerodrome measuring 800 yards by 900 yards". Levelling "such as to enable a Motor car to be driven across any part of the Aerodrome at a speed of 20 miles per hour" and draining would have been needed, and the Air Ministry would have granted a licence. This was confirmed at a meeting in autumn 1933 with a Ministry representative who thought it might be possible to arrange a golf course round the edge of the Moor, "so long as no bunkers were constructed at a distance of more than fifty yards from the boundary." Tall trees on the boundary would have been reduced in height, but not felled; and the proximity of the railway was not a problem: "Further, it might be an advantage in foggy weather". A small office building, where a telephone could be installed, and underground fuel tanks were envisaged; and "the Ministry would require to be satisfied that the public would not be wandering at large about the Moor both in the interests of pilots landing and the public themselves".

Money to finance the venture and the agreement of the Ministry of Health were both needed. In December 1933, in an interview with two representatives from the Ministry of Health, the Chairman of the Parks Committee and the Deputy Town Clerk were told the Ministry's view: the Micklegate Strays Act of 1907 provided that Hob Moor should be maintained as open space "so as to secure to the Citizens of York the full enjoyment of the same".

The aerodrome was not built.

Military Training

During the period 1912–20, an area of just over 1 acre, probably on Little Hob Moor, was used by the War Department for cavalry training. The Corporation was compensated by the War Office in respect of "loss and damage due to the military occupation of land on Hob Moor".

The Underpass

In 1918, under the Defence of the Realm Regulations, certain strips of land on Hob Moor, adjacent to the North Eastern Railway line, were to be taken by the Railway Company for utilisation as coal sidings. Land next to the cattle creep (underpass) was compulsorily acquired by the Military Authorities. In the Parks (NER Bill) Sub-Committee Minutes of 1921, details of the matters under negotiation are given. These included: proper paving of the existing underpass; a minimum height of 7' 6"; widening of the extension to the cattle creep; lighting the cattle creep by artificial light at night as well as by skylight; the maintenance of the road and the structure of the subway; and drainage work.

In 2002, a cycleway linking Acomb and the University was routed through the underpass. Concerns regarding this feature of the track included the lighting, floor, drainage, height clearance, and general appearance of the underpass ...

17. Hob Moor: Old Pastureland

HOB MOOR, ONCE PART of the very extensive commons outside the city, is now contained within the suburbs of the south-west part of York; nevertheless, it retains much of its traditional character. It is public open space, has fourteen access points, is criss-crossed by footpaths and has a cycleway passing through it, yet for many people it is glimpsed only from a distance and is not otherwise part of their lives. Those who visit Hob Moor can appreciate its space and its cloudscapes, and feel remote from the urban environment.

By late summer, the grass is parched a golden colour. In winter, shallow mists, quickly dispersed, form in the early morning, and evening fog rolls from the Moor into the adjoining streets. At all seasons, it can be breezy on Hob Moor but, especially in the first half of the year, calm days can be filled with the song of the skylarks.

This very special area is the result primarily of the continuing existence of the central Ancient Common, to which have been added adjacent areas. Apart from the episode of ploughing during the Napoleonic Wars, the central area has been pastureland from time immemorial; the added-on fields have been pasture since at least the 1840s and even the backfilled area of Kelsey's Pond has been pasture since the 1950s. Thus, the larger part of Hob Moor has the flora and fauna of old permanent pasture which has not been recently reseeded, treated with fertilisers or sprayed with herbicides.

Cattle still graze on Hob Moor from the beginning of May to the end of October each year (they were notably absent during the outbreak of foot and mouth disease in 2001). The

High summer on Hob Moor.

animals are up to six years old and some spend several summers on the Moor. Since no bull can be put on this public open space, all the cows are pregnancy-tested and only those in calf are depastured on Hob Moor. Some calves come too.

In the early part of the 20th century, things had been very different. In July 1916 the owners of milk cows on Hob Moor were required to discontinue milking their animals adjacent to the fence next to Tadcaster Road, in consequence of "complaints made as to the nuisance created there by the droppings from the animals". They were told to find a more suitable place for their purpose.

Sometimes cattle from an adjoining field strayed onto Hob Moor. In August 1918 Mr Allen was charged 2/6d per head "for trespass and damage" by twenty-one of his cattle, because his fence was defective. Later the same year, all the fences were put in order for sheep to be pastured during the following winter.

Both cattle and horses were depastured at times; in September 1921 the Golf Club asked that the horses be removed.

For the winter of 1928–9, cattle were put on the part of Hob Moor nearest Dringhouses (the fields next to North Lane) as an experiment. No rent was charged as the Corporation needed the cattle to eat or tread down the excessive amount of old fub grass or dead grass in this area.

Throughout much of the 20th century, there was generally an awareness of the number of animals depastured and the amount of eatage available to them. However, during the post-war period, in February 1948, the Corporation was told by the Government that Hob Moor was being inadequately grazed and that it should be used to the full for food production.

Cattle arriving at Hob Moor, 2004.

Hawthorn browsed by cattle, North Lane Pasture. (J M Tyszka)

In September 1941 it was decided that about 50 acres of the Knavesmire were to be ploughed out, with the cattle being transferred if necessary to Hob Moor, but there is no documentary evidence of any part of Hob Moor having been put under the plough, during either the Great War or the Second World War. This confirms the evidence of the flora and fauna today, which indicates that the area is old permanent pasture.

Hob Moor: Local Nature Reserve

In April 2003 Hob Moor was declared a Local Nature Reserve, the second such site in the York area, because of its important breeding populations of skylark and meadow pipit, its diverse flora, the leisure and educational opportunities offered by the area, and its ownership by the City of York Council. A post of Local Nature Reserves Officer, funded by English Nature, was created in order to ensure that the five-year management plan would be implemented, and on 17 May 2003 a very successful launch event was held at which the attractions included music, story-telling, jugglers, crafts, stalls, refreshments and guided walks to discover something of the history and ecology of Hob Moor.

The traditional use of Hob Moor has been as a pasture. This public open space now has football pitches and a permanent orienteering course, and informal recreation includes jogging and kite-flying, walking, exercising dogs, having a picnic on one of the logs, or just sitting and talking. With Local Nature Reserve status conferred on Hob Moor, there will be increased opportunities to help conserve and enhance its acres and to understand their ecology and history.

At the Local Nature Reserve launch event, May 2003. (P Walker)

18. *Flowers and Grasses*

ALTHOUGH FROM A DISTANCE Hob Moor may appear to be a stretch of unvarying, dull grassland, this is in fact far from being the case. One of the reasons for Hob Moor being a Local Nature Reserve is its rich diversity of flowers and grasses; different plant assemblages reflect the soil type and any reseeding in recent times. Open, cattle-grazed swards cover all of Hob Moor except The Triangle; Little Hob Moor is mostly amenity grassland, with some allotments and a small area which is being developed as a wild flower meadow.

The south-west area of Hob Moor (area A on the sketch-map), behind the Baths, is hummocky ground with variable soils consisting of a mixture of sandy and clayey loams. The swards here reflect the reseeding carried out after Kelsey's Pond was backfilled in the 1950s and are dominated by perennial rye-grass with abundant cocksfoot, rough meadow-grass and white clover. There is some buttercup, and nettles and creeping thistle grow in patches; annual cranesbills are found near the paths and common vetch is present.

The majority of the Moor (areas marked B) supports swards of greater diversity. The grasses present include meadow foxtail, crested dog's-tail, red fescue, creeping bent, cocksfoot and Yorkshire fog, with some occasional tussock grass and sweet vernal grass. Meadow buttercup, bulbous buttercup and common sorrel are abundant and there are patches of red clover and white clover. Occasional species include field woodrush, germander speedwell, meadow vetchling and yarrow; pignut is abundant towards the north-east part of the moor. There is creeping thistle, with some small patches of great burnet and some individual spear thistles.

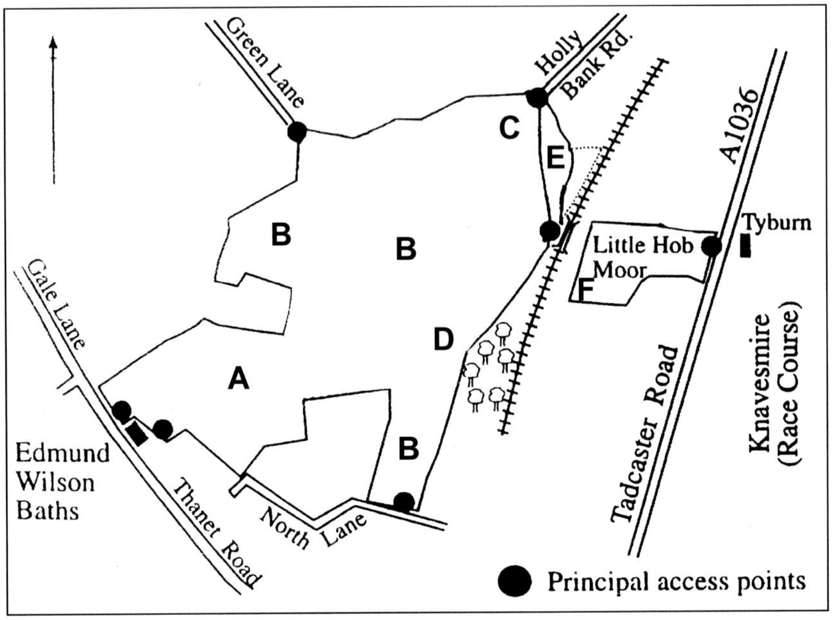

Flowers and grasses on Hob Moor and Little Hob Moor. Sketch-map showing the lettered areas mentioned in the text.

Tussock grass

Yorkshire fog

Common sorrel and bulbous buttercup
(J M Tyszka)

Meadow vetchling

Tormentil

Great burnet

Heath bedstraw

Sheep's sorrel

Dark mullein

Goat's-beard

Tansy

The soils of this large area of Hob Moor are mostly clayey loams, but in the north-east corner (area C) the soil is more sandy. Fine-leaved grasses like red fescue and common bent are abundant, and cat's-ear and harebell indicate less fertile conditions. There are patches of gorse also.

Near the eastern edge of the Moor, south of the underpass, is a similarly less fertile area (area D), supporting a rich diversity of flora including common knapweed, red clover and bird's-foot trefoil; tormentil thrives in small patches. This type of grassland was once very common throughout the country but is now rare.

The Triangle (area E) is a small area of acidic grassland, on sandy soil, and not grazed (except by rabbits). This very distinctive type of grassland is characterised by sheep's fescue, common bent and creeping soft-grass. The flowers present include sheep's sorrel, tormentil, great burnet and heath bedstraw. There are very few examples of acidic grassland in the City of York although there are extensive areas on Strensall Common.

On Little Hob Moor, in the corner (area F) south of the underpass, is an area which is not mown regularly and is not grazed, except by rabbits; the soil is relatively infertile. This area – part of the former brick-yard site – is now being developed into a wild flower meadow. In autumn 2001, plugs grown from seed of Yorkshire provenance were put in: oxeye daisy, self-heal, lady's bedstraw, betony, bird's-foot trefoil and cowslip. Following this, yellow rattle seed of local provenance was strewn. All these additions complemented the wild flowers already present, which included vetches, yarrow, dark mullein, tansy, red bartsia, teasel and goat's-beard.

As might be expected, the flowers on Hob Moor attract many butterflies. In the year 2000, the following were seen: small tortoiseshell, comma, ringlet, meadow brown, gatekeeper, small white, large white, red admiral, peacock, brimstone, orange tip. Peacock caterpillars have been observed on nettle plants, painted lady on spear thistle and, on The Triangle, cinnabar moth caterpillars on ragwort.

A Plant List is given on page 97.

19. Birds

ANOTHER REASON for Hob Moor being a Local Nature Reserve is that it has significant breeding populations of meadow pipit and skylark. The mown sports pitches and tussocky pasture, with scattered bushes, provide a mosaic of different grassland which forms an ideal habitat for these ground-nesting birds.

The meadow pipit is smaller than the skylark, being about 14.5cm (6") long as compared to 18cm (7"); both birds have rather sombre brown plumage but the skylark has a slight crest. Although visually the two species can appear similar, the songflights are very different: when a meadow pipit takes off, it appears to do so with difficulty, hesitating and then not rising far; it glides down with open wings. The skylark rises vertically, often two or three hundred metres, and then hovers for several minutes before descending vertically, singing all the while. It lands in the vicinity of its nest and then runs through the cover of the grass to reach it, unseen by predator birds. The nest is shallow and built in open, short to medium height grass, whereas the meadow pipit will build its nest in taller grass.

Recent surveys of the breeding territories of meadow pipits and skylarks on Hob Moor have shown that both species are well established. In 2000, there were at least ten breeding pairs of meadow pipit, the territories being both on the greater part of the main area of the Moor and on the south-western area between the Baths and Our Lady's School. In the same year, five breeding territories of skylark were mapped, with a further one being abandoned. In 2003, this number had increased to six, possibly seven; the increase may well have been due to the reduction in the number of sports pitches being mown, the felling of two stands of trees (one of which had failed) which had been planted near to the centre of the Moor, and a more appropriate regime regarding the cutting of the thistles. Skylarks usually start singing

Skylark. (Chris Gomersall, RSPB)

Carrion crow. This stand of amenity trees was felled in order to extend the area available to skylarks, a priority species for conservation as in recent years there has been a drastic decline in numbers nationally.

on Hob Moor some time during January; their breeding season extends from April to early August and they avoid nesting within 100 metres (100 yards) of tall trees, as these provide excellent perches for predator birds, principally carrion crow and magpie. Thus, their breeding territories are more closely grouped around the centre of the Moor than are those of the meadow pipits.

Of course, many other birds can be seen on Hob Moor. Kingfishers visit the becks; linnets and other finches feed on the thistle seeds; common and blackheaded gulls loaf on the mown areas from autumn through to spring; wrens sing loudly in the boundary hedges; kestrels and sparrowhawks hunt frequently; and The Triangle area is particularly important, especially for whitethroat, blackcap, garden warbler and bullfinch. Swallows and house-martins are seen in their feeding flights from April to October, with swifts also present from May to August; the open sky above Hob Moor is the ideal place to observe these birds in large and small numbers. Also, although there has recently been a steep decline in numbers of starlings, they are abundant around Hob Moor, due to the combination of a large area of permanent pasture where they can feed on invertebrates and houses and gardens where they nest and feed on scraps. In addition, there is a small but regular roost of corn buntings which gathers in winter in grass tussocks and bushes.

Thus, there is much on the Moor to interest the bird-watcher. For many people, however, the skylark is the most important bird, its song being the spirit of Hob Moor.

Birds seen on Hob Moor

For ease of reference, the lists are arranged in alphabetical order.

Regular sightings

Blackbird

Bullfinch

Chaffinch

Crow, Carrion

Dove, Collared

Dunnock

Fieldfare

Goldfinch

Greenfinch

Gull, Blackheaded
  Common

Jackdaw

Kestrel

Linnet

Magpie

Mallard

Martin, House

Pipit, Meadow

Redwing

Robin

Rook

Skylark

Sparrow, House

Sparrowhawk

Starling

Swallow

Swift

Thrush, Mistle
  Song

Tit, Blue
  Great
  Long-tailed

Woodpecker, Great spotted

Wood-pigeon

Wren

Yellowhammer

Less frequent sightings

Blackcap

Bunting, Corn
  Reed

Cuckoo

Dove, Stock

Goldcrest

Heron

Kingfisher

Merlin

Snipe

Wagtail, Grey
  Yellow

Warbler, Garden
  Willow

Wheatear

Whitethroat

Woodcock

20. Hedgerows

ALTHOUGH HOB MOOR is first and foremost an area of traditional pasture, its boundary hedges are of considerable interest, offering an invaluable wildlife habitat.

Untended hedges, that is to say those that have increasing breadth and height (as do many of those on Hob Moor), offer food, shelter and breeding sites to various fauna including plant-feeding insects, those that live in leaf litter, and certain small mammals. An untended hedge also acts as a highway along which animals can move at minimal risk from predators. For birds, taller hedges provide song-posts and nest-sites at a suitable height, including dry hollows in dead trees.

Each insect has specific habitat requirements and the greater the number of species of shrub in any hedge, the greater the number of species of insects. In Britain, hawthorn alone supports 150 species of plant-eating insects, an exceptionally large number. Hedges which

Elder

Blackberry

Hawthorn

are not trimmed, and which therefore flower freely, attract butterflies, bees and other insects that feed on nectar and pollen. Both plant-eating insects and the larvae of butterflies and moths fall prey to a wide variety of predator species which in their turn are victims of others.

Hedges, especially those whose characteristics more closely approach those of woodland, offer a suitable breeding habitat to birds. Hawthorn is particularly well patronised; overall, in Britain the most common species breeding in hedges are robin, song thrush, blackbird, chaffinch, whitethroat, dunnock, and yellowhammer. Because the shrubs are exposed to the light, those allowed to grow naturally produce a heavier crop of berries than those in woodland, and birds visit this larder frequently.

If one stands at the centre of Hob Moor and looks at the boundaries, it is easy to see that there is an abundance of untended hedges! There is an obvious predominance of hawthorn, or May-tree, but closer inspection reveals that some are species-rich. Thus, the hedges on Hob Moor offer a very significant contribution to the overall ecology of the Moor.

Around Hob Moor, hedges run along the beck sides, usually on one side only but sometimes on both sides. It would appear that originally there was a hedge on each side, perhaps to stabilise the banks and at the same time prevent animals from falling into the ditch, and that lengths have been removed on one side, probably for ease of access for maintenance of the ditch, in relatively recent times. Indeed, there are references in the Parks Committee Minutes for 1933 concerning the felling of trees along the beck. The Drainage Board was

Hawthorn and buttercup: the May spectacular on Hob Moor. (J M Tyszka)

Species-rich hedge between Hob Moor and North Lane Pasture.

stated to have chopped down "dozens of large thorns" but the Board contended that there had been no undue interference with the trees and bushes at the side of the beck and that all the work done was necessary for the proper cleansing of the watercourse. Also, it is known that trees and bushes were lost during major works on Holgate Beck in the 1980s and replacement trees planted.

An additional intermittent hawthorn hedge runs down the centre of North Lane Pasture, following the curved line of the medieval field-strips. In the 1950s, this hedge had tall trees of other species at intervals along it. In contrast to the hawthorn hedges, there are two lengths of species-rich hedge. The first of these is along the eastern boundary of The Triangle and contains coppiced hazel, English elm, willow, ash, crab apple, elder, holly, oak and blackthorn as well as hawthorn. The second is between Hob Moor and North Lane Pasture and includes English elm, hawthorn, blackthorn, dog rose, elder and, on the north side next to the beck, guelder rose, which is particularly associated with old hedges. It has a flower-head of pale cream flowers; the tiny central ones are surrounded by larger, five-petalled infertile ones. The leaves are maple-like and toothed. There is also an apple tree which is possibly a hybridised Beauty of Kent and a reminder of the 19th century adjacent orchards.

Although hedge-dating is a subject of much debate, it is generally agreed that the greater the number of species, the older the hedge (unless a multi-species hedge has been planted originally), and studies have revealed that, for a sample 30m (100') length, each species represents approximately a hundred years of age of the hedge. The two species-rich hedges mentioned here are both along very old boundaries of Hob Moor; the one between Hob Moor and North Lane Pasture is marked on Samuel Parsons' map of 1624 (see pages 26-7), and the rule of thumb gives the age of the hedge as being in the region of 600 years.

Along the beck separating Hob Moor from The Triangle, between the Holly Bank access and the underpass, the hedge contains alder, ash, beech, dog rose, elder, English elm, wych elm, hawthorn, holly, sycamore, willow and yew.

The hedge along the northern boundary of the Moor contains a predominance of hawthorn but also ash, blackthorn, crab apple, elder, English elm, wych elm, holly, poplar, silver birch, yew and some garden shrubs. The oldest trees in this hedge, however, appear to be some willows and, interestingly, there is a reference in the Acomb Manor Court Rolls in 1651 concerning repairs to the highway between Cowlainegate and Willow Bridge. Cowelane is mentioned also in 1603 as leading to Hob Moor, so it seems that willow trees have been a notable feature on the northern boundary for a very long while.

Willow tree on the northern boundary of Hob Moor.

21. Trees

THE BOUNDARY HEDGES of Hob Moor are well-established; in two cases, they are very old features of the landscape of Hob Moor. By contrast, the tree-stands and individual trees are more recent, in some instances much more so.

The hawthorn trees, both as single specimens and in groups, are self-set; some of them have grown from small bushes since the 1940s. Near the hawthorns by the Green Lane access to Hob Moor, there is an English oak tree of which the top has been taken out at some stage. The size of the trunk and of the branches indicates that it must have been a much taller tree and that it may be up to 200 years old. Just outside the access gate is the huge stump of another oak tree, felled some time ago just above ground level and now producing new growths. Perhaps these two trees are the modern descendants of the "Hobbe Okes" mentioned twice in the Acomb Manor Court Rolls in 1557? Those "Okes" must have been impressive features in the landscape of the Common. The only other oak trees growing on the area of the present-day Hob Moor are some young ones in the boundary hedge on the east side of The Triangle. Also at the Green Lane access, there used to be an imposing group of mature elm trees; they were felled in 1982, having become diseased.

At the Holly Bank access, there are two splendid beech trees. In the 1950s there was an avenue of at least five beeches on either side of the path; they were half the height of those which now remain. It may be that those that remain are the sole survivors of a small "plantation" which existed here in the mid-19th century. Two were removed during the 1982 beck management works.

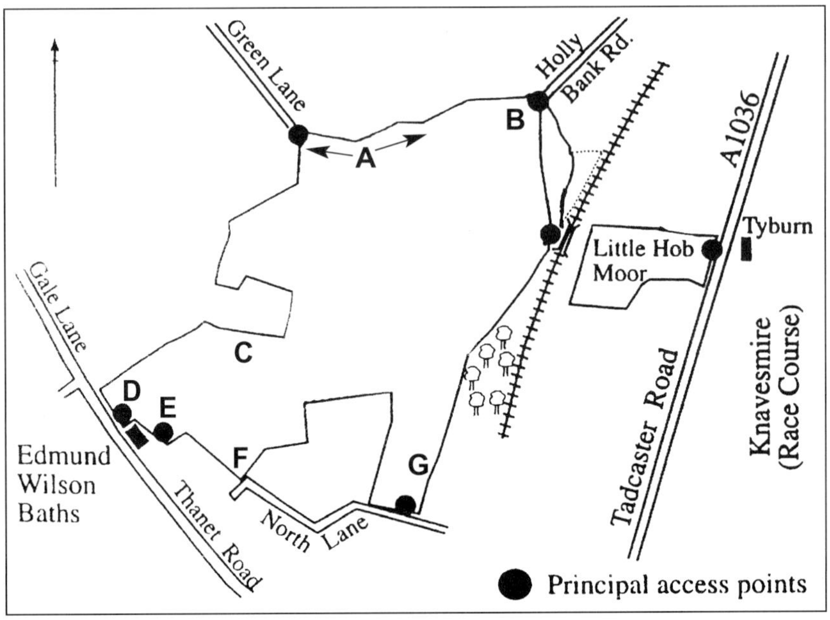

Amenity trees on Hob Moor. Sketch-map showing lettered areas mentioned in the text.

Since 1982 so-called “amenity” trees have been planted on Hob Moor. Although they could well be considered to be unwelcome intruders in this traditional pasture, they are certainly not without interest.

Along the northern boundary are various single trees and groups of trees planted in 1983–4 to compensate for the trees and bushes lost during the drainage works carried out by the Marston Moor Internal Drainage Board during 1982. In area A on the sketch-map, they include decorative ash (with one claret ash, which has dark red leaf-stems and dark red leaves in autumn), horse chestnut, a stand of eleven hybrid elms (developed for their disease resistance after Dutch Elm Disease had wiped out so many elms), and a group of three decorative maple, of which one is a Caucasian maple. Further along to the east, in area B, there are sycamore, ash, red chestnut, horse chestnut, lime and another stand of decorative maple. The beautiful Black Italian poplar near the Holly Bank access was apparently planted at about the same time.

In area C on the sketch-map, outside the fence along the southern boundary of Our Lady’s School, is a group of trees including Norway maple, several horse chestnut and red chestnut, lime, ash, Italian alder, willow, rowan and an old cherry. In area D, between the Baths and Kingsway West, and in area E, behind the Baths, plantings done in 2002 and 2003 included common oak, rowan, hornbeam, beech, whitebeam, ash, sweet chestnut, London plane, field maple, silver birch, crab apple and sessile oak. These trees were added to those already there, including Italian alder, horse chestnut, silver maple, cherry, field maple, sycamore and ash.

Trees along the northern boundary of Hob Moor. From left to right: hybrid elms, a Caucasian maple with willow behind, the two beeches at the Holly Bank access, the Black Italian poplar, and a hawthorn beside the cycleway.

Alder and horse chestnut in late November

Ash

Bird cherry

Norway maple

By the North Lane/Jervis Road access to Hob Moor (area F), there is a group of ornamental trees, two of which are spectacular when in flower: Norway maple and bird cherry. Willow and rowan complete this group. Along the edge of North Lane Pasture, in area G, there is a line of field maple and one rowan.

Thus, on Hob Moor there are at least twenty-five species of amenity tree. On Little Hob Moor there are yet more!

At the side of Hob Lane there are ornamental cherry planted at intervals along the whole length, with other species including hawthorn, English elm, ornamental hawthorn, a young

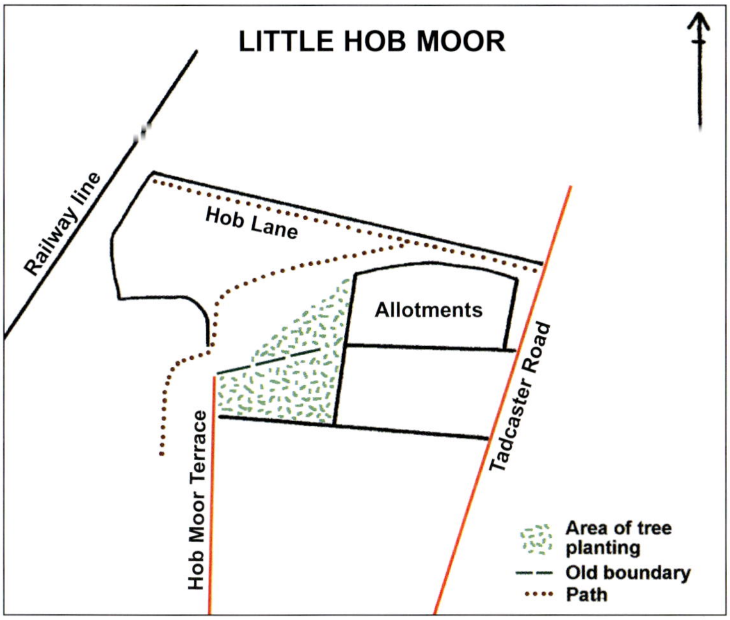

English oak, elder, sycamore, domestic apple, dog rose, holly, and garden shrubs along this boundary of the area. Along the boundary with Tadcaster Road is a row of mature horse chestnut and, in the trimmed haw-thorn hedge which bounds the allotments, some mature Lombardy poplars.

In the area between the allotments and Hob Moor Terrace, some most interesting trees have been planted in recent times amongst mature trees; the result is a parkland which is a delight to the eye, especially in autumn. The trees here include three species of decorative ash, field maple, common oak, lime, sycamore, rowan, decorative cherry, laburnum, ornamental hawthorn, Norway maple, sycamore, purple-leaved plum, hybrid whitebeam, poplar, a large decorative maple and an ornamental crab apple.

An old boundary runs part of the way across this area: there is a boundary bank with several old ash, willow, hawthorn and Lombardy poplar along its length. Continuing the line of the bank there is a very large silver birch, with an old ash tree nearer to the allotments boundary.

Little Hob Moor: the boundary bank and parkland beyond.

It is noticeable that in the planting carried out on Hob Moor in 2002 and 2003, native species predominate. Native species are those which were established in Britain without human agency, before the land-bridge with continental Europe disappeared when the English Channel was created by a rise in sea level after the end of the most recent period of glaciation. They include, in the order in which they arrived: juniper, aspen, bay willow, hazel, small-leaved lime, bird cherry, goat willow, wych elm, rowan, black poplar, yew, whitebeam, crab apple, wild service tree, hornbeam, silver birch, Scots pine, common alder, English and sessile oak, ash, holly, hawthorn, white and crack willow, wild cherry, field maple and beech. Of course, not all these are found now in the York area.

Other species arrived later: walnut was introduced by the Romans, as was sweet chestnut; sycamore was introduced in the Middle Ages. These three are naturalised, that is, they behave like native trees, maintaining themselves indefinitely without human intervention, and have widely invaded native vegetation.

Other more recently arrived trees are called "exotic" and were imported usually as seeds but in a few instances as a single plant. They include: horse chestnut introduced from Albania in 1616; Lombardy poplar from northern Italy in 1758; Black Italian poplar from France in 1750; Italian alder from southern Italy and Corsica in 1820; common laburnum from central and southern Europe in 1560; and silver maple from North America in 1725. Norway maple had arrived by 1683 and London plane is a hybrid first planted in England in about 1680.

One of the most striking features of a tree is the appearance of its bark. There is an immense variety but its function is the same in each case: it is the outer, dead layer of the trunk of the tree; it is waterproof and protects the underlying tissues from drying out and also against attack by fungi, bacteria, insects and larger animals. Some trees have thick, deeply fissured bark; some bark is very smooth; some peels; some is pitted. The trees on Hob Moor and on Little Hob Moor offer a very interesting selection, both of texture and colour.

Whatever the season, there is always some aspect of the trees on Hob Moor and Little Hob Moor to enjoy: their different "skeletons" in winter; frost-covered catkins; next year's buds already formed as the leaves fall in the autumn; the glorious autumn colours; the fresh greens and bronzes as the various species come into leaf in sequence in the spring; and in summer, one can of course sit in the shade of the single hawthorn beside the main track, near the middle of Hob Moor, and enjoy the song-flight of the skylarks.

Texture and colour of bark

Cherry

Oak

Beech

Black Italian poplar

22. *The Becks*

HOB MOOR IS PART of a large, flat area drained by a network of becks and ditches, parts of which are now culverted. However, the full pattern can be seen on the 1852 6" Ordnance Survey map (see page 45) and includes a stream along the western edge of the Ancient Common area, with an arrow indicating that the flow was from north to south. This streamline is still visible as a shallow ditch, water-filled after a period of heavy rain; a photograph of this feature can be seen on page 10. The line both on the map and on the ground seems straighter than those of the other streams around Hob Moor; it truncates the medieval ridge and furrow in Hob Moor Field and may have been straightened at some stage after its creation. It is interesting to observe that Samuel Parsons on his map of 1624 draws this western boundary as a straight line between the Moor and Stanes Close, and that Francis White, in his map of 1785, shows the same stream as a gently curving line, quite different from the other streams. He also shows a short beck flowing from the centre of Hob Moor northwards to Holgate Beck. This former streamline is still visible on the ground.

The present-day drainage of Hob Moor would appear to be straightforward: Moor Drain joins Chaloners Whin Drain which flows from Askham Bog through Dringhouses; by the Holly Bank access, this stream is joined by Holgate Beck and the water continues northwards to the Ouse at Acomb Landing. However, all is not as it seems! This is indeed how the drainage developed, but it underwent massive changes in 1968 and 1982.

Francis White, 1785: Part of his Plan of the City of York and Ainsty (enlarged), showing the drainage of Hob Moor and the area around. (York City Archives)

Former tributary of Holgate Beck, Hob Moor, looking north.

A short distance to the south of the underpass, Chaloners Whin Drain goes through a screen, which catches any debris, and then down into a large chamber from where it is diverted into a culvert under the Knavesmire. The scheme allows for a small flow to continue northwards throughout the year, thus ensuring that the beck between the underpass and the Holly Bank access does not become stagnant. This diversion was created by the City Council in 1968. At that time, the Foxwood area was being developed and Holgate Beck was carrying extra flow as a result from the Foxwood Culvert; to balance this increase, flow was taken out of the system by diverting the water of Chaloners Whin Drain before it reached Holgate Beck.

A second scheme, the Holgate Beck Flood Alleviation Scheme, was implemented in 1982 by the Marston Moor Internal Drainage Board. As implied by the scheme's title, this was designed to minimise the flood risk within the catchment during periods of flood-lock due to high water levels in the River Ouse and localised flooding due to the peak rates of flow in Holgate Beck. The scheme was also intended to reduce the rate of flow in Holgate Beck which at times was flowing fast and at depths of at least 1.2m (4'), which was dangerous and caused bank erosion. Works were carried out on Holgate Beck along the northern boundary of Hob Moor and the Hob Moor Diversion Culvert was put in so that the water flowing in the Foxwood Culvert was now diverted across to the chamber by the underpass and thus also into the Knavesmire Culvert.

Another element of this major scheme was the installation of a flood-control chamber on Holgate Beck in the north-east corner of Hob Moor. The chamber contains a double-height weir which, when raised, blocks the flow north to the Ouse and diverts it southwards along Chaloners Whin Drain; the flow along the Drain is thus temporarily reversed as far as the Knavesmire Culvert Diversion Chamber by the underpass. This was done in November

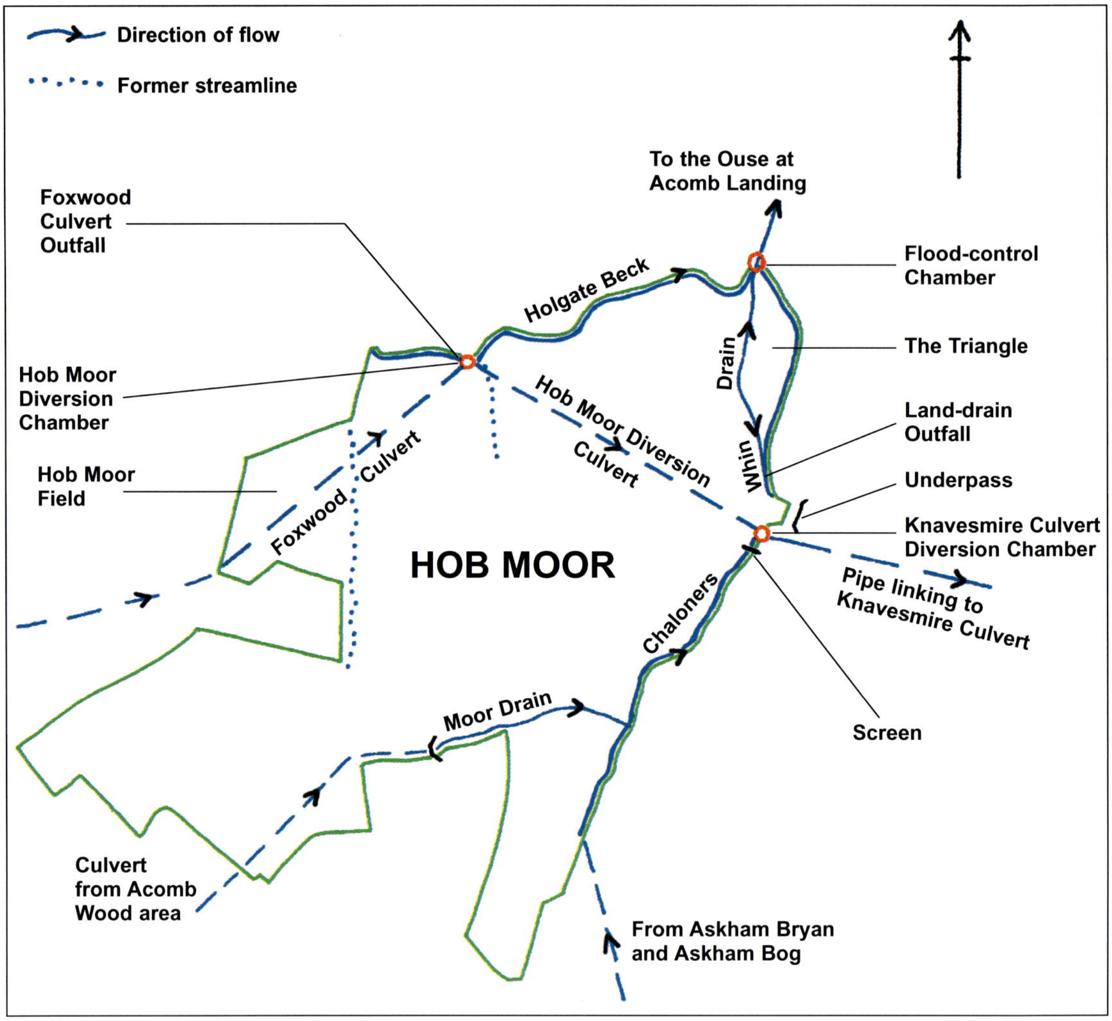

Sketch-map showing drainage features of Hob Moor.

2000, when a flood period coincided with a period of heavy rainfall in the Holgate Beck catchment area. It is also done when work is being carried out downstream of Hob Moor. The disadvantage of the raising of the level of the weir is that the water-level in Holgate Beck along the northern boundary is also raised; the banks become saturated in time and then there may be slippage, as happened in November 2000. Remedial work was then required to stabilise the banks and to ensure that the flow of water was not impeded.

There is also a land-drain system under Hob Moor; it outfalls into Chaloners Whin Drain, halfway up the bank, a short distance north of the underpass.

Thus, Chaloners Whin Drain is diverted at all times via the Knavesmire Culvert into the Ouse between the crematorium and Bishopthorpe Palace, and Holgate Beck can be diverted along the same route when necessary.

Bank slippage on Holgate Beck, Hob Moor, after the heavy rains of November 2000. (G Berwick)

Remedial work in progress, Spring 2001.

Meadowsweet, between the underpass and the Holly Bank access.

In times of heavy rain and especially following high winds, personnel from the Drainage Board can be seen monitoring the state of the becks around Hob Moor, and they carry out annual bank mowing and dredging of the becks in order to ensure unimpeded flow of the water. Their maintenance of the watercourses by mechanical means is the modern equivalent of work which has been carried out by hand for centuries to combat silting up and bank slippage.

A document of 1639 gives details of "paines" or fines imposed upon the villagers of Dringhouses and there is frequent mention of scouring the water courses and "gripping" the land, that is, putting in small ditches. In 1659, Thomas Smyth, William Forbut, Robert Dorkwray, George Allen, Elizabeth Hood and Mr Henry Breary were all fined for "not scouring waterway". There is a record for the Manor of Dringhouses in May 1829 concerning work to be done by various people: of the Pasture Masters of Micklegate Ward, it was required that "their Ditch adjoining the North Lane be sufficiently scoured and cleansed; That the whole of their Ditches between North Lane and the Bottom of Cherry Garth be sufficiently deepened scoured cleansed and widened – and that their watercourse leading from Mr Dalby's Brick Yard to Acomb Watercourse be also sufficiently deepened scoured cleansed and widened". (At the time, the area now known as The Triangle was called Cherry Garth.)

In the 20th century, work continued to be done by hand. In the Minutes of the Parks Committee for September 1922, there is reference to recent heavy rains having caused the sides of the beck on a portion of Hob Moor to fall away; the Head Gardener was to do the work necessary. In 1945–6 lengths of the becks were deepened by groups of Italian prisoners of war. The becks have been maintained by machine since the early 1960s.

Aquatic plants found in the becks include common duckweed, fool's watercress and water-starwort; marginal plants between the underpass and the Holly Bank access include yellow iris, figwort, celery-leaved crowfoot and lesser celandine, and abundant meadowsweet grows on the banks. The flora alongside North Lane Pasture is a mixture of woodland, streamside and grassland species, for example, male fern, pendulous sedge, wood false-brome, enchanter's nightshade and greater burnet saxifrage. Three-spined stickleback are the only fish present in Holgate Beck, but kingfisher are seen quite frequently, flying along the becks. On the whole, the wildlife interest of the becks around Hob Moor is somewhat limited: there is scope for enhancement of this habitat.

23. *Future Management for Wildlife*

IN 1996, THE CITY OF YORK carried out a Biodiversity Audit, a review of all the sites in the area of the new unitary authority, in order to describe the state of the natural environment in the City of York and to plan a Nature Conservation Strategy. As a result, Hob Moor was identified as being a "Wildlife Site", later called a Site of Importance for Nature Conservation. This designation indicated that Hob Moor was significant ecologically in the city-wide context and worthy of protection. In 2003, it became a Local Nature Reserve, the second such site in the York area, because of its important breeding populations of skylark and meadow pipit, its diverse flora, the leisure and educational opportunities offered by the area, and its ownership by the local authority.

Statements of the wildlife interest of Hob Moor had been made in the Biodiversity Audit and, together with recommendations for its conservation, in a report written in 2000 by Martin Hammond for the Friends of Hob Moor. Also, the City of York Council commissioned an ecological report in 2000, in response to proposed cycleway development on the Moor. Some of the recommendations had already been implemented when, as part of the application procedure for Local Nature Reserve status, the future management of the area was set out more formally in a five-year management plan which was submitted to and approved by English Nature.

Weeding, from the Luttrell Psalter, circa 1335. The weeds appear to be thistles and their removal necessitates the use of substantial gloves and long-handled implements – a familiar strategy! (By permission of The British Library; Add. 42130 f172)

The plan was written by the City of York Council's Countryside Officer and included a site description, management review, aims, management objectives, and a management prescription which contained details of proposed operations for each of the five years. Two maps were appended, the first showing the status of the site in spring/summer 2002 and the second being a projection of the desired status of the site in March 2008.

The Aims of the Plan

1. To maintain or increase populations of skylark and meadow pipit
2. To ensure the longevity of unimproved herb-rich grassland communities
3. To maintain and enhance biodiversity
4. To conserve heritage
5. To raise awareness of the natural environment and heritage issues throughout the community
6. To provide the opportunity for safe informal recreation in a semi-natural landscape
7. To maintain and enhance visual amenity.

The Management Objectives

Biodiversity

1. Modify grazing regime to achieve a fine mosaic of grasses of different length between close-cropped and 25cm
2. Cut and remove arisings from key grassland areas which cannot be grazed
3. Rationalise use of sports pitches and amend cutting regime accordingly
4. Manage injurious weeds and other undesirable plant species to optimise grazing potential and habitat diversity
5. Implement a programme of wildflower plug translocation in appropriate locations
6. Manage existing species-rich hedges and restore boundary hedges in key locations
7. Rationalise and maintain amenity trees to optimise ground-nesting habitat
8. Reinforce and extend gorse thicket in appropriate locations
9. Modify management of drains and becks.

Archaeology

1. Ensure that management operations do not damage the fabric of archaeological features present on the site.

Interpretation and Access

1. Establish a programme to interpret the ecology and heritage of the site using a variety of media
2. Establish a formal education programme based on ecology and heritage in accordance with York Leisure Office practice
3. Implement a campaign to encourage responsible use of the site, focusing on fly tipping, dog fouling and access
4. Carry out regular inspection and maintenance of footpaths, cycleways and access points.

Research

1. Investigate and implement, where appropriate, management agreements on peripheral sites not in the freehold of the City of York Council
2. Carry out regular collection of ecological and visitor use data to monitor the effectiveness of management.

(Excerpts of the management plan reproduced by permission of City of York Council.)

Starting in summer 2003, early work included increasing public awareness of the site, thistle and ragwort control, a reduction in the number of pitches being mown, litter collections, discussions initiated with Marston Moor Internal Drainage Board in order to enhance the beck environment for wildlife, mowing of The Triangle and removal of the arisings, the preparation of material for use in schools, events and practical tasks for schoolchildren and the general public, monitoring of bird populations and a first visitor survey.

Little Hob Moor is not included as part of the Hob Moor Local Nature Reserve but nevertheless, improvements to the habitats are being implemented. Wild flower plugs grown from seed of Yorkshire provenance were planted in the area of the former housing in autumn 2001, and yellow rattle seed strewn. It is hoped to enhance the thicket adjoining the wild flower area by some additional planting of native species such as field maple, hawthorn, holly, crab apple and purging buckthorn; the latter may encourage brimstone butterflies to breed.

The five-year management plan is a detailed expression of intent to manage Hob Moor for wildlife, to conserve archaeological features, and to promote informal recreation and educational use of the site. Only the future will tell how successful the conservation measures have been. Hob Moor is in a large area (the Vale of York and the South Pennines) which is subject to high levels of nitrate deposition from the atmosphere. The soil-enrichment which this brings, together with the accelerating pace of climate change, will in the longer term most probably result in significant changes in the flora and fauna of Hob Moor.

Holgate Beck, northern boundary of Hob Moor. This length, where ground elder predominates, is an example of where it is hoped to increase biodiversity.

North Lane Pasture. The trees along the central line running down this field are the remnants of an old hedge and the five-year management plan provides for its restoration as a double-row hedge in year 2 or 3.

Cowslip on Little Hob Moor. Introduced to this area in 2001, the cowslips have thrived. It is planned to introduce cowslip in colonies on the former mown pitch areas on Hob Moor. It will be an element in recreating species-rich grassland as it is one of several interesting species mentioned in plant records for Hob Moor dating from 1879.

24. *Reminiscences of Hob Moor*

HOB MOOR HOLDS SPECIAL MEMORIES for many people, some of whom have talked informally to members of Friends of Hob Moor or written about their memories of the Moor between 1930 and 1970. Some were "born on Hob Moor", meaning that they were born in dwellings which have now disappeared: a tin bungalow and three small cottages near Kelsey's Pond and the cottages on Little Hob Moor. Some lived very nearby, others further away but often crossed the Moor when going to visit relatives in other parts of York, or were amongst those who came to Hob Moor to picnic. Many people used to cross the Moor on the way to work and very large numbers walked across it on Race Days.

There are fond memories of Kelsey's Pond, especially the bulrushes, so beautiful but often out of reach. One youngster used to gather bulrushes at Christmas and take them to a chemist in Gale Lane who would pay half a crown for twelve and use the fluff inside as a snow effect to decorate the shop windows. In the spring, the children used to collect frogspawn and take it home in jam jars. Later on, there would be thousands of tiny frogs, thumbnail size, which would abound on the paths. One lad used to sail on the pond in an old iron bathtub; sometimes waterhens' eggs would be taken and cooked to eat. One memory was of an outing: "One morning very early, when it was still misty, Mr Kelsey took me out in his punt to show me a golden carp, near the middle of the pond. He'd wrapped sacking round the oars and lifted them clear of the water and then glided to the right place; we saw the fish."

"The ponds were a lovely place to walk around, birds, wild flowers and tadpoles were there just like a nature reserve, with only a few houses in those days."

"It was the best playground anyone could ever have."

There are many reminiscences of other wildlife: water voles in Chaloners Whin Drain, kingfishers, large dragonflies, barn owls, and cuckoos which were usually heard for the first time towards the end of April. There were fewer magpies and collared doves than there are today. The youngsters used to look, always unsuccessfully, for skylark nests and dig up pignuts to chew.

The lads would talk to a tramp whom they came across and who might be cooking up a rabbit stew; the tramp would let them dry their clothes following a failed attempt to jump across one of the becks. One tramp used to watch the ponds and tell the boys about the submarine that came up at night! The boys used to enjoy trainspotting near the underpass where they would "dally for hours", identifying the different liveries and seeing (and smelling) the black steam engines shunting the rolling stock in the Dringhouses Reception Sidings. They played cricket on a small area, specially mown for them by the friendly golf course greenkeeper, near the Green Lane access; and they used to be paid at the clubhouse for any golf ball found in the "rough", the payment depending on the state of the golf ball concerned.

One event which left a strong impression was the forced landing of a military aircraft on the Moor. A 'plane was such a rare sight in those times that the children were fascinated and some did not return to school at the end of the dinner hour. Those that did so arrived late and were punished; those who stayed on the Moor got off scot-free, which caused lasting feelings of injustice in the pupils who had returned!

Some of the lads who lived in the Holly Bank area were very familiar with the Moor and identified certain areas and features by name. Thus, there was Kelsey's Corner, Dringhouses Corner, the Fairy Ring (a circle of hawthorn bushes, now an incomplete circle of hawthorn trees), Little Moor (The Triangle), The Jungle (most of Little Hob Moor, which was totally overgrown in the years after the Second World War), and The Sandhills (the area near the Holly Bank access): "The Sandhills area was our seaside."

After the golf club removed to Pike Hills in 1946, the children would play in the sandy banks around the green on The Triangle, and in the becks: "The beck on Holly Bank side was a place where children paddled and dug sand when school was out, when I used to walk there."

"Hob Moor for me in boyhood days was a place of magic, for the sun always shone and the sky was always blue, or so it seemed, over Hob Moor. The Moor was a place of pilgrimage, often for the whole family, including grandma and grandpa, for it was the destination of our Sunday afternoon walks ... After Campbell Avenue, the adventure began for, between two of the few houses which had then been built on Hob Moor Drive, there was a little ginnel which led to a wooden plank bridge over Holgate Beck. Then came the thrill as the expanse of Hob Moor opened up before me. Freedom!"

"I remember Hob Moor fondly as a magical place, never believing the stories my elder brother and sister told me about Hobgoblins and the like."

"Hob Moor was our kingdom, our domain. We would set off at nine o'clock in the morning with our sandwiches and an orange drink, and we wouldn't come back till seven in the evening. Our mothers would be calling to us from the gate in the corner."

Holgate Beck, the northern boundary of Hob Moor, photographed by Frank Oates in 1947.

25. Past Present

TO BE ON HOB MOOR is to feel connected to the past. Reminders of the lives of previous generations are there for all to see: the boundaries of the Ancient Common; the medieval and Napoleonic cultivation strips; the old causeway; in the distance, the Minster, built on the site of the Roman legionary headquarters; the low banks around the former golf course greens. On Little Hob Moor there are the patterns in the dry grass where the old cottages used to be; the Hob Stone; and, most poignant of all, the Plague Stone. But we can "see" Hob Moor with other eyes, too.

Hob Moor: A Mysteriography

Until now, not nearly enough has been written about the natural history, the geology, the history and archaeology of Hob Moor, those most sublime and unappreciated acres of the York landscape. And nothing at all has been written about Hob Moor's mysteriography – its contribution to the mythic experience of our ancestors.

The mysteriography of Hob Moor has been all but lost, yet fragments of it are recoverable and these still have the power to bring enchantment into our lives. The channels of enchantment are simple: Hob Moor's spirit of place, its flora and fauna, its canopy of sky, as well as its silences, strange mists and fearful darkness. All these were familiar to our pre-industrial ancestors, whose lives were more precarious than our own and who were involved in a constant struggle for survival. And without the benefits of calendars, clocks and modern technology, they had to turn to other things for guidance. They believed that nothing was without significance. Everything had meaning and, above all, it was the connections between things that were important and pointed the way to a divine order of life.

So it was that the appearance of Orion in the night sky marked the end of the pastoral year in November and its disappearance in May heralded the beginning of summer. So it was that when the wrens fled through the hedgerows at the midwinter solstice, the people knew that the wren's Lord, the Holly King, was being killed by his brother, the Oak King. So it was that at the midsummer solstice, when the great oaks on Hob Moor – the Hobb Okes – were crowned with a sudden flush of green, this was a sign. The Holly King had returned from eternity to kill the Oak King and the oaks were bearing witness to the seasonal cycle of life.

The mysteries of Hob Moor are yours. You can take them back, find others, share them with those you love – and with tender hearts cherish what she has so graciously given us.

Stephen Sayers

Robin and Wren. (Swea Sayers)

The Friends of Hob Moor

THE FRIENDS OF HOB MOOR GROUP was set up in October 1999 and became a registered charity in January 2001.

The Objects of the Association are, in brief:

1. to work in collaboration with others to promote the conservation, protection and improvement of the natural environment of Hob Moor
2. to promote Hob Moor as an open space amenity for education, recreation and leisure-time occupation
3. to promote research into the history and ecology of Hob Moor, such research to be made available to the public.

Activities of the group include:

planting wild flowers
producing leaflets
stalls at local events
archaeology
surveys of flora and fauna
guided walks
illustrated talks
litter-collecting
walks and talks for members
newsletter for members
exhibition – history and ecology of Hob Moor
helping to implement the management plan

THE FRIENDS OF HOB MOOR
Caring for Wildlife and Heritage
Reg. Charity No. 1084566

The walk on 20 July 2003, led by Mark Tyszka, to look at butterflies and flowers. Members and non-members of the Friends of Hob Moor participated.

Hob Moor and Little Hob Moor:

A list of plants observed by members of Friends of Hob Moor during 2001–03

Alkanet, Green
Apple, Crab
Ash

Balm, Bastard
Balsam, Himalayan
Bartsia, Red
Bedstraw, Heath
Betony
Bindweed, Greater
Bittercress, Hairy
Bittersweet
Blackthorn
Bluebell, Spanish
Bramble
Brome, Soft
Bryony, Black
 White
Burdock, Lesser
Burnet, Great
Buttercup, Bulbous
 Celery-leaved
 Creeping
 Meadow

Campion, Red
 White
Cat's-ear, Common
Celandine, Greater
 Lesser
Charlock
Chervil, Rough
Chickweed, Common
 Upright
Cinquefoil, Creeping
Cleavers, Common
Clover, Red
 White
Cocksfoot
Corydalis, Yellow
Cowslip
Cranesbill, Cutleaved
 Hedgerow
 Small-flowered
Cuckoo Flower
Currant, Flowering

Daisy
 Ox-eye
Dandelion, Common
 Lesser
Dead-nettle, Red
 White
Dock, Broad-leaved
 Clustered
Dog's-tail, Crested

Elder, Dwarf
 Ground

Feverfew
Figwort, Water

Goat's-beard
Golden-rod, Canadian
Goosefoot, Green
Gorse
Groundsel

Hair-grass, Tufted
Harebell
Hawksbeard, Beaked
 Smooth
Hawthorn
Herb Bennet
Herb Robert
Hogweed
 Giant
Honeysuckle
Horsetail, Field

Iris, Yellow
Ivy
 Ground

Knapweed, Black
 Greater
Knotgrass
Knotweed, Giant

Lady's Smock
Lettuce, Wall
Lords-and-ladies

Mallow, Common
 Musk
Marigold, Corn
Marram
Mayweed, Pineapple
Meadowsweet
Medick, Black
Mouse-ear, Common
Mugwort
Mullein, Dark
 Great
Mustard, Garlic
 Hedge

Nettle, Stinging
Nipplewort

Orchid, Bee

Parsley, Cow
Pellitory of the wall
Pignut
Plantain, Greater
 Ribwort
Poppy, Opium
Primrose, Evening
Privet, Wild

Radish, Horse
Ragwort, Common
 Oxford
Raspberry
Rattle, Yellow
Redshank
Rose, Dog
 Guelder
Rush, Soft

St John's Wort,
 Perforate
Sandwort, Fine-leaved
 Thyme-leaved
Saxifrage, Burnet
Self-heal
Shepherd's Purse
Silverweed
Sneezewort
Sorrel, Common
 Sheep's
 Yellow
Sow-thistle, Prickly
 Smooth
Speedwell,
 Common Field
 Germander
 Lilac Ivy-leaved
 Thyme-leaved
Spurge, Broad-leaved
 Sun
Stitchwort, Greater

Tansy
Tare, Hairy
Teasel
Thistle, Creeping
 Spear
Timothy
Toadflax, Ivy-leaved
Tormentil
Trefoil, Bird's-foot
 Lesser

Valerian, Common
Vetch, Bush
 Common
Vetchling, Meadow

Watercress, Fool's
Willowherb, Great
 Rosebay
 Square-stemmed
Woodrush, Field
Woundwort, Hedge

Yarrow, Red
 White
Yorkshire Fog

Thanks

WE WISH TO ACKNOWLEDGE the help given by many people, including the following:

Aspects of history

M Bailey, G Berwick, M Carbert, R Dalton, the late Mrs Dent, T Gates, B and M Gittos, J Howarth-Pulleyn, the late J Kaner, P Lankester, D McCloy, C Mennell, M Newsome, A Sinclair, I Tomlinson, K Wheater.

Aspects of ecology

M Cresser, B Hickman, A James, D McCloy, J Noak, B Potter, R Stirk, G Wallbanks.

Reminiscences

M Bowes, D Braithwaite, E Brown, A Carbert, T Dalton, K Jackson, Mr Noble, C Plowman, C Ravensdale, B Robson.

Technical assistance

P Wilson and V Coxon at Dringhouses Library, the staff at Micklegate Post Office, C Appleby, M Heddon, P Walker, C Wheater.

The staff of the following organisations have always responded most willingly to our requests for information and help:

The Borthwick Institute of Historical Research, The British Library, London, City of York Council (Environment and Development, and Education and Leisure Departments), City of York Reference Library, English Heritage, King's Manor Library, Marston Moor Internal Drainage Board, On-Site Archaeology, Pike Hills Golf Club, St Mary Bishophill Junior Church, University of Reading Rural History Centre, University of York Department of Archaeology, York Archaeological Trust, York Art Gallery, York Castle Museum, York City Archives, York Cricket and Rugby Union Football Club, York Minster, Yorkshire Archaeological Society, Leeds, Yorkshire Museum, Yorkshire Wildlife Trust.

Hob Moor. (P Palaeologina)

Select Bibliography

Please note that a full list of the books and articles used in the preparation of each chapter has been included with the copy of the book in the City of York Reference Library and the York City Archives.

Anderton, B, and Green, R, *Holgate Windmill, York*, Holgate Windmill Preservation Society, 2003

Backhouse, J, *The Luttrell Psalter*, The British Library, 1989

Backhouse, J, *Mediaeval Life in the Luttrell Psalter*, The British Library, 2000

Baddily, R, *The Life of Dr Thomas Morton, Late Bishop of Duresme,* 1669

Bennett, H S, *Life on the English Manor 1150–1400*, Cambridge, 1937

Benson, G, *An Account of the City and County of the City of York*, republished by SR Publishers Ltd, 1968

Bogg, E, *Lower Wharfedale and round about the old city of York and the Ainsty,* 1904

Boylan, P, *The Ice Age in Yorkshire and Humberside*, Yorkshire Museum, 1977

Brown, S, *Stained Glass at York Minster*, Scala, 1999

Buttery, D, *West of York in Times Past*, Countryside Publications, 1982

City of York Council, *Local Nature Reserve Management Plan for Hob Moor*, 2003

City of York Council, *Local Plan – Deposit Draft,* 1998

City of York Council, English Nature and Hammond, M, *Biodiversity Audit*, 1996

Drake, F, *Eboracum*, 1736

Elgee, F and H W, *The Archaeology of Yorkshire*, Methuen and Co, 1933

Evans, J G, *The Environment of Early Man in the British Isles*, Paul Elek, 1975

Fitter, A and Smith, C J, *A Wood in Ascam*, Sessions Book Trust, 1979

Hall, R and Ottaway, P, *2000 Years of York,* York Archaeological Trust, 1999

Hammond, M, *Hob Moor: an assessment of its wildlife interest and recommendations for conservation management – a report for the Friends of Hob Moor,* October 2000

Hammond, M, *Proposed cycle path development at Hob Moor, York: ecological report for the City of York Council,* 2000

Hammond, M, *A Register of Green Sites in York,* Nos 16 and 17, Yorkshire Wildlife Trust and York Natural Environment Trust, 1991

Hey, D, *The Oxford Companion to Local and Family History,* Oxford University Press, 1996

Hodgson, G, *Holgate – a History in Five Parts,* part 2, published by the author, 1999

Hutchinson, J and Palliser, D M, *Bartholomew City Guides: York*, Bartholomew, 1980

Knight, C B, *A History of the City of York,* 1944

Mabey, R, *Book of Spring Flowers* (Flora Britannica), Chatto and Windus, 1998

Mitchell, A, *A Guide to the Field Trees of Britain and Northern Europe*, Collins, 1974

Muir, R and N, *Hedgerows: Their History and Wildlife,* M Joseph, 1987

Murray, H, *Opportunity of Leisure: The History of the York Railway Institute, 1889–1989,* York Railway Institute, 1989

Murray, H, Riddick, S, and Green, R, *York through the Eyes of the Artist*, York City Council, 1990

Nichols, J, *The History and Antiquities of the County of Leicester,* 1795–1815, Vol 2, part 1, reprinted by S R Publishers

Nisbet, W W M, *The Strays of York and their Management through the Ages*, undated

Nuttgens, P (ed), *The History of York, Yorkshire,* Blackthorn Press, 2001

Palliser, D M, *Epidemics in Tudor York,* Northern History, Vol 8, 1973

Pettinger, B E, and Stirk, F R A, *Marston Moor Internal Drainage Board: Holgate Beck Flood Alleviation Scheme,* Association of Drainage Authorities' Gazette, 1986

Phillips, R, *Grasses, Ferns, Mosses and Lichens of Great Britain and Ireland*, Pan Books, 1980

Pocock, M H, *Halfdan's Heritage – the story of Dringhouses AD 876–1998*, Saint Edward the Confessor Church, Dringhouses, York, 1998

Purkiss, D, *Troublesome Things – A History of Fairies and Fairy Stories*, Penguin, 2001

Rackham, O, *Trees and Woodland in the British Landscape*, Dent, 1976

Rackham, O, *The History of the Countryside,* Dent, 1986

Reader's Digest: *Field Guide to the Birds of Britain*, 1981

Reader's Digest: *Field Guide to the Wild Flowers of Britain*, 1981

Reader's Digest: *Field Guide to the Butterflies and other insects of Britain*, 1984

Richardson, H, *A History of Acomb*, Yorkshire Philosophical Society, 1963

Royal Commission on Historical Monuments of England, *An Inventory of the Historical Monuments in the City of York*: Vol 1: Eboracum, Roman York, 1962; Vol 3: South-west of the Ouse, 1972, HMSO, London

Rushworth, K, *Pocket Guide to Trees*, Mitchell Beazley, 1980

Syson, L, *The Watermills of Britain*, David and Charles, 1980

Taylor, C, *Fields in the English Landscape*, Dent, 1975

Taylor, W B, *A History of the Tadcaster-York Turnpike*, York Historian, Vol 12, 1995

Victoria History of the Counties of England: *The City of York*, 1961

Vince, J, *Discovering Watermills*, Shire Publications, 1987

Wacher, J, *The Towns of Roman Britain*, Batsford, 1974

Wenham, P, *The Great and Close Siege of York 1644,* Roundwood Press, 1970

Whitworth, A, *Yorkshire Windmills,* Rigg Publications, 1991

York Group for the Promotion of Planning, *The Strays and Ways of York,* Sessions Book Trust, 1968